THE BOOKS OF AMERIKA

Book I

A TOWN OF JAMES

A Comedy and Play

For the Theatre of the Mind

By

Joseph Eldredge

Annotated, with a forward by the author

CHOICE
PUBLICATIONS

Cover design by Joseph Eldredge
Set in Times New Roman font
Printed in the United States of America

ISBN 979-8-9882132-0-8

For my family…

CONTENTS

FORWARD

This book tells the story of two brothers, twins, one born into poverty, the other into prosperity, both by chance bearing the name of 'James'. Yet in this most are they the same: the James' are in love with a widowed maid, Marigold.

Where else then than onto Jamestown, our earliest English (American) colony, plant them? Therefore, in this book we may examine our own American History.

This is not entirely a play, nor entirely a novel, nor entirely a script. It seeks to steal from the bests of all these three, in a unique reading experience. Dialog is usually in iambic pentameter, though prose is used for certain characters, and the action-line descriptions. The language of our characters is based on the Restoration period in which they are imprisoned, and so some footnotes have been added.

I offer my book to you as dear dreams told to old friends. Hear in that spirit. As to any offense, I can only plead my case and attest, that I write not to appease but to please.

PROLOG – DAWN OF AMERIKA

Listen, with the beginning, Amerika was without form. There was only Atlantic, flowing, rolling everywhere. Then a mound, pregnant with Earth, rose from the deep, was apart the deep. And SAHM was there, is in the mud, made all forms, moulds with his hands the mounds the formed, forming Country.

There were no people in all that country, except for those Indians. They were already there. SAHM was lonely; he called over the seas. There was no echo. He waited for so long, that in an evening he fell down asleep. The sleep lay long on SAHM – his own mud covered him; he's buried deep. Nobody woke him.

Winds over the salt and sea. Galleons cut the Atlantic flood. Wanderers from the East, they're nosing West. Smell of gold. Led by the nose. In an early morning they land on Amerikan land. There were no people on it. Except for those Indians.

So they bound themselves into a people, like a tower they rose and raised a town of straw and slime. It was a Jamestown. There were no James' there yet.

ACT 1

NOVEMBER THE 8TH 1674 – NIGHT

Hear, another Galleon westward bound. Ship's bell of bronze, it rings in the night, bounding o'er the dark of the waters of the deep. Led by the ear, snoring on its deck, the sleepers are sprawled. One stands, is awake, stowaway, renegade on the bow. Ey lowers eir high brow, looks to all the dark of the deep, eir voice there, an echo back here.

IOSTAF
(*aside*)

This is a play first in a series three,
A history unfolded in slant decree,
I am Iostaf, singer and narrate Knight,
Of time and gender-joined, a chanting sprite,
I push and plash into innermost ear,
Let in all John-a-Dreams and hear! Upon
This ship we start our play, to stage a rage
The founding of a nation Amerikan.
Let play perform from sign to eyes to mind,
Read on, two curtains fall to see design.

A passenger lurched to deck to upchuck his gut. He spilled

over the side. Iostaf shrank to a gnat's size. In the chucker's

hat ey hid, bobbed there. Ey whistled lounged winked & said:

IOSTAF

(*aside*)

We sail for a town rich in James', I share

A Jamestown full of James', there's where

I'll present plays, of masters, servants, and slaves,

Rouse themselves on destiny's manifesting[1] waves,

There's where tobacco smoke's a currency,

And rich widows rule a widowcracy[2],

The indentured choke under a trammel[3] hand,

While freemen gorge grog with no plotted land,

Where Algonquins and Tribes welter and bleed,

While the greedy flame their jimson weed,

And visions of SAHM's conquest do foresee,

Among such hearts black we stage Comedy,

And sail into a November discontent,

Bacons and Berkley's vie for power unpent,

The Town's breaking into two in dissent,

Twins warring in belly tearing torrent!

---

[1] Manifest Destiny is a phrase first used by the American and Jacksonian journalist, John L O'Sullivan, in 1845

[2] a government ruled by widows

[3] entangling, as in a net

Ey shouted in pain and changed into a man made in armored plate to glitter under the moon. He lanced airy foes upon the jousting deck to unseat his rivals. Victor, he ventured below, turning him to her his maiden her prize she treks under hammocks, jungles of hammocks, to find James Joiner asleep. She stroked his hair, soothing dreams, and so she soothsays:

> IOSTAF (AS JOUST MAIDEN)
> (*aside*)
>
> Asleep James Joiner my first of the Twins two,
> His mother's perished, his father's grave'd too,
> He is a man from birth apart his other,
> His Twin separated, James Drugger's his brother
> Who in Jamestown owns a plantation wealthy,
> He's rich, yet he's poor, and there's my comedy.

She morphed to the shape of Francis Drake. He leveled his bright sword on the chest of the man strung up in slumber beside James Joiner, Ferdinando black and bright Maroon[1].

> IOSTAF (AS FRANCIS DRAKE)
> (*aside*)
>
> Here on bedside beside's a daedal belamy[2],

---

[1] an escaped slave; of a runaway slave community
[2] good friend

A friend to James, he's free from slavery,

Hearen me, here I name, Ferdinando,

In the Great Dismal Swamp his family grow,

To them he turns to slake[1] their claim of exile,

But betricked to servanthood he'll be guiled,

For all Amerika come trade in years,

A break in bond and they'll chop both your ears,

For tobacco must grow, its smoke must flow!

*He turned again to Iostaf. Ey leaned atop the crow's nest. Ey
leaned down over the river. The Galleon sailed up the James
River. Jamestown's shone, ahead, glowed with dawn.*

IOSTAF

See, to a beginning new we do land,

One grand project, my Amerikan brand,

With which I burn,

Amerikan darks, Amerikan lights,

These I bring, indraught from my ocean nights,

So sun will rise,

My day will break,

Let these rhymes end,

When this my rime begen, now,

Now burst intwo young flames my Town of James!

---

[1] to render less painful

JAMESTOWN – AT THE DOCKS

Now the shore was a vice. The ships were full of sick. They could not leave until they had pledged seven years of life in servitude. So some died on the ships. Among these ill contents, James Joiner and Ferdinando, starved to serve, were let on the shore, the sand-ditched harbor of Jamestown.

They were led from the busy harbor to a marketplace to a purple curtained booth. James Joiner and Ferdinando waited. The curtain opens: John Pot, a young man, pale, rich, wide, wearing his wooden booth like a skirt. He smokes and drinks.

JOHN POT

You art bonded to me you cattle'd men,
I'll souse my pad with this indentured pen,
See, with this pen, I imprison your years
To labor towards my ends. After this term,
You will grain a portion of my cash crops,
Crops of corn and some tobacco bushel'd,
With which you may smoke, plant, or sell well,
With this, purchase a pygmy of my plot
To husband as your own, with this, may marry
A mistress, or mar your oats in bachelorhood,
To me it matters not. Now sign your names,
Or mark with a swart sign if write you can't.

JAMES JOINER
(*bemused*)

Ferdinando, what sign use you, remind.

FERDINANDO
(*bemused)*

Why, James, mine is the sign of the pleaseman,

For wouldn't it please this wide want-wit to mark

A samlet[1] on his bargain mephitical,

Like an unliterate would gladly wag

To jab that mark, thus mar his life all to job.

JAMES JOINER

And by this devil wager your soul take

To till his earth to 'ternity or grave.

Come now, oh wide one, hawker of kickshaw[2],

Let's see the contract, hand it to your hands.

They take the contract, reading it both, then look on John Pot.

JAMES JOINER

Why does he wear his booth?

FERDINANDO

To buoy him o'er the boatloads of his bull.

JOHN POT

What? What!?

---

[1] a salmon symbol was used by some Northeastern Native American tribes to sign treaties with British colonies

[2] something ridiculous; trinkets; unknown food

15

FERDINANDO
(*to James Joiner*)

I'll show our captain and boat both that his

New mates're first rate by reading aloud, lend

Hand to me, hand, and hold.

JAMES JOINER
(*holding the contract up*)

Hand does.

JOHN POT
(*puffing angry smoke*)

Humf!

Hmm!

FERDINANDO
(*warding off smoke; reading aloud*)

What White trade winds prevail from you, master!

This contract decrees a servant shall slave

In seven year degrees, to the labor

Of his master, to his whims, to his favor,

And may be dismissed, traded, beaten, banged

Bought and battered on the whims of the master.

In addition, shall he also be baked?

If the servant is of a complexion

Darker than the bill of a mainland rooster

At 3 o'clock of the morning in a

November month – o' how efficiently

Specific, sir! – then this servant's term will

16

Be extended by the length of two years,

– Unless that complexion shift to the light hue

Of an old grey hen's bum feathers in moonlight

Of an April month when the evening rain

Has glittered to silver all the black sons o'day

– In this case the once cock'd servant shall his

Nonce master croak, his high role usurp,

To adulations of all branded birds' chirp!

– So says, John Pot, Tobacco Baron, man

Of the people and their persons, of the

Family of the founders of Jamestown,

Motto, 'Never without Master' – never

Without mustard, mustiness, bake, cake, and

Chickens!

JOHN POT

Nay, that addendum I did not approve…

Nor the motto's amend becomes this me.

Sign it now… if you can.

JAMES JOINER

Ferdinando, if I could not write, what

Sign would I mark?

FERDINANDO

          A beer pot foam'd to hops,

You'd mark a James brave by brandy. Or sign

Shape of open eye, who works but when watched,

Eyeservant James! But first,

JAMES JOINER

The contract's uneven.

JOHN POT

You have no choice but to mark years, so sign.

Or back to boat to sprout scurvy you go.

I don't care for the marks-

JAMES JOINER

-But you've flammed[1] us,

O wide master butter! See, you've marked here

For me service of seven Laban years!

Seven years long for this springing young goat!

But uneven's in'this, *nine* life-turns you'd take

From friend Ferdinando[2]!

JOHN POT

So? So? Thou art

My bond. If you'd not bound to me, then 'cure

Ye a passage back to ugly England.

FERDINANDO

Sooner time trendle[3] than re-fare fatefull seas,

Yet I like not this unfair trick, like a

---

[1] tricked;

[2] the years of indentured service are assigned based
on a new, Amerikan concept, 'Race'

[3] to wheel backwards

Babe by its father's drabbing botched, the World

New made has dragged to shore its vice of Old.

JAMES JOINER

This skirted con greets us at Old's hell-gate!

Our musty master is much impartial,

He's uneven as his brains to his scuttlebutt[1].

JOHN POT

(*covering his drink; fuming smoke*)

Sign the contract and lease the years of life,

For its for your freedom here that you work,

Yet wary be, my servants may be whipped.

FERDINANDO

Our just desserts-

JAMES JOINER

-Our pot luck, the servants have been served,

Let's sign to be whipped, then baked, sold and bought,

Fear the fare not, for

I'll buy your unhonest years when I'm free,

Then we'll eat the glazed cakes of liberty!

They signed their years away. John Pot branded their earlobes. He gave them directions to his plantation far up on the Neck, be there. He bobbed off, his booth like a wide boat.

---

[1] a keg of drinking 'water', used on board ships

JAMESTOWN – MAINSTREET

Jamestown was a-jumble with men. There wasn't a woman in sight. Tobacco smoke was all thick and afloat the grounds chimneyed out the buildings dingy beachy cheap cluttered full of grog full of men. In the center an empty stone church; a man is in the stocks at its door a beer pot hangs off his neck.

James and Ferdinando walk up, look on him with pity.

JAMES JOINER

Ferdinando, methinks our new blobber[1]

Master will whale us to the dirt, for not

A single carpenter,

FERDINANDO

Or glover[2],

JAMES JOINER

We see,

FERDINANDO

Which are our professions... All's tobacco.[3]

JAMES JOINER

We'll be steered into the leanest of beefs!

---

[1] archaic form of 'blubber'

[2] one who fashions gloves

[3] the planting economy excluded diversification of trades

FERDINANDO

Dirtied in such peculiar institution,

Dirt itself become, soiled by slavery,

Our Spirits ebb, crust, stone, toil to soil…

Dame Marigold Mammon blonde young widow arrayed in finery livery glided to the two and without even a wink slapped James Joiner wide across the cheek – downing him.

MARIGOLD MAMMON

James! James, you cod, you catch of gander shank!

Woman's trickster, think ye' my honor will

Wear out, fade as an in-demand doorknob?

Get up! Get up! Mud-man!

Ferdinando laughed deeply. James Joiner marvelously confused muddy-messed stood up. He rubs his eyes.

FERDINANDO

James the Conqueror his conquests return,

Despoiled and armed for the countera-slap.

JAMES JOINER

Madam-

FERDINANDO

-Beldam

JAMES JOINER

-I assure you

FERDINANDO

-Assay you

JAMES JOINER

-That we've never met

FERDINANDO

-Out the curtain of bed.

MARIGOLD MAMMON

Who's this wheezing oat, James? Your slave?

FERDINANDO

His
knave.

JAMES JOINER

How do you know my name? Or face so well

To hosanna it so by palms?

FERDINANDO

Handshake hit.

MARIGOLD MAMMON

Play dumb, James, and *you* mime it well for him,

You scratching catpipe, you, you

FERDINANDO

-Charming clicker.

She raised her fanning hand. Ferdinando yelps chuckles and
ducks. James and Ferdinando surrender to Marigold.

FERDINANDO

Madam, do not hurt us, but humor us!

Since you did not greet me with pecking smack,

I see you and me are not *we* just yet.

So play the lamp, and enlighten me.

MARIGOLD MAMMON

James the Jobbernowl can introduce me.

JAMES JOINER
(holding his cheek; shouting)

This' the wicked ponk that on nights haunts

swamps-

-Fanned he fell into mud again.

FERDINANDO

Sir, when on the ship you said you'd kiss earth,

I didn't think you'd mean a strumpet of her.

(to Marigold)

He's beslubbered in his mud-rudeness now, maid.

MARIGOLD MAMMON

Let him lie there when he lies here. My name

Is Marigold, once married to a man

Mammon, planter of some corn, but most smoke.

He kissed her hand.

FERDINANDO

Ferdinando, simple servant to'my James.

MARIGOLD MAMMON

Tell your master James of Mud, 'if amends

He'd make, at Deaf John's Tavern I will wait.'

23

Exit Marigold her perfume laced the air all lilac a lady leading. Ferdinando looked on after her.

JAMES JOINER

First foot on a New World and I'm fallen in mud.

FERDINANDO

You'll rise from mud richer than cleanest Duke.

James stood and Ferdinando helped to clean him off.

JAMES JOINER

However so?

FERDINANDO

You have hooked a widow.

JAMES JOINER

She's mistaken-mudded me for another,

Another James, who looks yet not likes like me.

FERDINANDO

Some hidden twin? Some doppler? Matters not,

Her mistake is your rich take, claim you'd stake

Upon her mine, to take what's hers for mine.

JAMES JOINER

Ha! To wed her before the trick's unbed'd?

FERDINANDO

Aye… her deep-rooted love's radicate, planted

By some wooing sower, we'll pull up radish,

We'll reap all the growths of his husbandry…

Widows of this town I've heard are wickedly

Rich, what for all the weddings they've re-vowed,

For men live not long here, on such frontiers,

You as her husband, rich planter, will pay

Off our lock-purse master, thus manumit[1] us

With wedding night's fittus!

JAMES JOINER

What fine wittus!

Cheerfully arm in arm they go looking for Deaf John's.
Exeunt. Quiet all. Smoke suffuse the mind stage. Iostaf
Transfigured Knight appears, leans on church's steeple.

IOSTAF

So our Amerika begins on a con,

While these hounds hunt for the Tavern Deaf John,

I my watch will rewind, and time re-clock,

To read how Marigold was stoked to sock

A James brother she thought was his other!

The race will run!

Confusion will catch the Truth by its heel,

So is my town of James! Read on and hear!

Adam   Thorngood   grizzled   grey   an   old   peddler   of
kitchenware wheeled his cart to Townsquare. He looked up.

---

[1] to liberate from slavery

ADAM THORNGOOD

Will you now be turning the time for me?

IOSTAF

Yes, I'll be!

ADAM THORNGOOD

Then into my otherguise

I'll slip, ready to meet inheritrix[1].

He wheeled off his pots and pans a'clamor as Iostaf spun counterclockwise along the steeple ey laughed like a new morn babe ey played like a young flame playing an old game.

IOSTAF

(*turning back time*)

Now I'll shake the ol' scene,

And reel back this play's screen,

Time will a trendle turn,

Like Greeks spun out their urn,

I'll shift to go-between,

And sing more than I seem,

That old leaves will re-grow to fresher green!

---

[1] female inheritor of great fortune

THE PLANTATION OF JAMES
DRUGGER – EARLIER MORNING

James Drugger owned a tobacco plantation of a thousand acres, manned by servants and slaves. Cold, tall, his house hid behind a wide wall; James lived there, by his big garden and his screening trees.

Enter Dame Marigold Mammon, bundled warm for the morning cold, walked to the gate of the plantation. There is Adam Thorngood, his pots and pans brought to sell to James.

MARIGOLD

Good morn, Adam.

ADAM THORNGOOD

Morn, good madam.

MARIGOLD

What do you?

ADAM THORNGOOD

Madam, I wake in morning, and my needs

I relieve, both bladder and hunger aches

And all the wants I work for wallet's sake,

For the first, find a spot driest to dew,

For second, steal eggs, or for a breakfast begs,

Third, I thrift these cheap pots, or hock some pans

That not well the campfire's heat withstands,

And so when all my morning needs are met,

I joy in idle, liking my joy to music,

27

I march to the panpipes, waking as'I play,

The fairies, sprites, or native spirits that

Slumber un-serenaded in unpeopled

And old grey woods above the Neck, there's where

The New World's creatures remain to be named,

The birds of air, beasts of field, early as'Eden

They wait for me to seek and wake, all kinds

I find in the ungardened frith[1].

MARIGOLD
(laughs pleasantly)

       Adam,

What do you at the gate?

ADAM THORNGOOD

      Madam, I do wait.

MARIGOLD

Adam, there we're paired! James should be here if

He has hospitality... Such guests, such

Warm guests on a cold morning's threshold makes

Waiting a wickedness.

ADAM THORNGOOD
(*winking*)

      Tis pleasantness.

A round Garden grows by the spoke of us.

---

[1] a woodland

She smiled at him and offered her hand.

MARIGOLD

Tell me, Adam, how till here a garden

Midst such a wilderness as surrounds us?

ADAM THORNGOOD

Our old Adam is unfallen at all!

I've such tale to you tell! When one

Morning cold wandered I in holtes hoar[1]

I heard on high a hollering, as though

Some elf of Spring, or immigrated gnome,

Called down to me from a rig[2] his greeting,

Bounding, his bellows from branch to branch went,

Like some sparrow's dalliance breeding,

Far I followed, into forest's deeper part,

I obeyed, as though to be bewitchéd,

For hours I'was led, until any way out

Was long ago forgotten and end,

Lost in thorn and bramble, I mused despair,

But the call did muse to me, further yet, far yet,

So went I onward, cutting ways through the

Total brakes, cutting myself with the brakes,

But broke through, I found a most magic sight,

---

[1] old, grey, magical forest
[2] a slanting twig; the back of the body

An orchard, wild forest become Garden,

The trees were stood to widest avenues,

As though the strolling ground of old Giants,

T'was Old Indian land, those Gardeners

Genius who with their brands did burn the trunks

Improper away and out their design,

For they willed their trees to root wide apart,

Wide 'nough for three carts to travel abreast[1],

So I found that all there in forest's heart,

Was as a man-cured park, a mended Nature,

Or Nature's nurture on and of itself,

Mind mending on Man,

A space of sound's healing,

That seemed the very shape, shade, and bower

Of Paradise refound by the techniques' power.

MARIGOLD

Say on, Adam, this is a tale I like,

That more's told in its manner than its main,

This rich speech shines more in the speaking

Than a thousand and one flashes of plot

Or fashion could keep a queen in quiet

Through thousand and one nights.

---

[1] according to Adam, what colonists called
wilderness was, to the Natives, a manicured park and
mythic paradise

ADAM THRONGOOD
(*acting out the tale*)

Enchanted, enchanted I roamed there among

The pillar'd trees arranged in stately pomp

More perfect than of ancient Parthenon,

Yet more ancient, yet more early, were these

Architectures of man-mended-nature,

For the trunks were older than stone, yet the

Architraves were grafted with buds of Spring

That shade'd cool my walk in heat of day,

And reflected me, garland'ed in the

Numerous silver pools that under that

Generous canopy lay low, a'nod,

And would have summoned me to slumber as them

When I had gazed into their watery

Mirrors, when without malice, like my Eve looked,

But there my face being old, white, manish,

Haha! Ah! Marigold! What I could tell!

Oh how un-Eve'd's this Adam now, without

His pair, his twin his wife his half his theme

That sleeps in her bed'd earth, ready to rouse,

But that her champaign shall not up to him

All her rolling, bubbling wine and fine bread

I'd bring balance to bear to this half-pair!

31

Adam was turning into Iostaf — so he slowed himself down,
sat on the ground and shook as an old man too excited –
Marigold put her hand on his shoulder.

MARIGOLD

Are you alright, Adam?

ADAM THORNGOOD
(*mournfull*)

What circles are we that want...

I'm sorry, I'm sorry, to tale turn again,

My messenger showed himself to me...

I saw him in one of these pools, he'd landed on a

branch behind and above me, from above he said-

A morning bell announcing the Master James Drugger was
walking to the gate.

ADAM THORNGOOD
(*quickly whispers into her ear*)

Madam, blossom'd on branch of ympe-tree[1], he,

The sprite that led me,

On this tree, shining golden in Spring's change,

Was a most wise and Barred Owl, who hooted

To me his message to thee.

---

[1] fairy tree, where revelation is granted to gadding
knights on quests for grails

MARIGOLD

What'd he hoot?

ADAM THORNGOOD

(*imitating owl call*)

Who-cooks-for-you, who-cooks-for-you-all!

IN THE GARDEN OF JAMES
DRUGGER – CONTINUOUS

Enter James Drugger, shooed Adam out and ushered Marigold in, where they walked arm in arm along the unsown furrows. Adam shrunk to a grasshopper's height and followed them in secret, winking to you.

James Drugger was a rich man who dressed plainly, dirty with garden, even like an indentured servant. He was identical to his brother, James Joiner, but for a few scars on his left foot.

He carries a bundle of plucked radishes o'er his shoulder.

They stand under the barren apple tree.

MARIGOLD

James, our marriage would your claim most enrich.

JAMES DRUGGER

What claim is that, my Marigold?

MARIGOLD

Your claim's

Upon my heart, James, worth more than all New
World's gold.

JAMES DRUGGER

Hm! Marigold I'd marry gold,
An unmalleable thing when to woman's heart
Compared. I think you marry to have another
Husband to husband, reven[1] up your land-hoard.

MARIGOLD

Why do you say this? Why torment my heart?
Why does my heart in yours so long to melt?
Yours is so ill, it suspects ill in mine,
Then my heart would ill in yours become,
Till I suspected e'ery stranger a robber,
Every friend a foe, every love a lie...
James, I'd only take what's been robbed from me:
My stolen heart retakes the heart that took.

James Drugger shivered turned his back to her.

MARIGOLD

What wounded you, James? I'd mend all wounds.
It's no great leap of faith to take the hand

---

[1] to steal, take, or confiscate; or, to ruin, or destroy

Of widow so faithful, and wooed by you,

Even wooed against your wanting – I'm stuck,

I'm trapped with you in your trap of nothing,

Your beckon of a turned back, your call cross,

The snares of soft hands, the catch of cold eyes,

All your yes' that yell in eyes above lips' noes.

Walk with me to the market today, please.

JAMES DRUGGER

No, you won't find me there. I've business

With Nathaniel Bacon.

Slowly, she walks away to leave. James turns touches her.

JAMES DRUGGER

But wait, wait, I've another time to trap

With you in nothing, and imprison us,

Your hand in mine – come inside, nothing's home,

But may be us.

MARIGOLD MAMMON

I'll not till a wedding.

He let go her hand.

JAMES DRUGGER

Well, tomorrow call on me again, then,

My Marigold nothing, and maybe I'll

Find a trust in you-

MARIGOLD

-You're a fanged cat!

You toy with me your prey!

She stalked off angrily. He watched her go.

James Drugger straggled through his tobacco fields his garden alone. He leaned under his lone leafless apple tree.

JAMES DRUGGER
(*internal*)

A corpse in a copse[1] of trees. Winter trees

Rake the sky, clean the clutter of a few clouds.

Under the crust of their ice there's a faith,

Under the bark, the phloem, within warm sap,

Their religion readies to worship Spring.

My blood is not so pious a devote.

I am a frostman, winter tundra's me,

Of no faith, but Seasons' immortality.

ADAM THORNGOOD
(*aside*)

This James brother was grown a bit crooked,

He's grafted wicked with rods of riches,

To Marigold he yearns to yield, but first

He'd buy her best gold as loyalty's proof,

---

[1] a small, dense woodland, managed by coppicing

As though under sheet were hidden touchstone[1],

So's distrust that from youth on throne was grown.

Enter, Nathaniel Bacon, standing black-garbed black brim-
med his dark face in the shade; he seemed to hover subtly
over the field over the furrows to the apple tree to the man
with the furrowed brow.

NATHANIEL BACON

James Drugger, good morning to you.
JAMES DRUGGER

Nathaniel…
NATHANIEL BACON

Jamestown dogs are starving in the cage, James.

On servanthood's scarce smoke they feed.

Their own free field to grow they need.

But more than this, that there's mission divine,

'Grow tobacco' our all-Giant bellowed,

We've all heard him, under the tavern floor,

When his frame shakes this New World quakes,

The tobacco must grow, its smoke must flow…

Now Bacon stood so close to James that he sat him down on
a stool under the tree and he stood over him.

---

[1] a small tablet of dark stone, used for trying precious
metals by rubbing and observing the trace there left

NATHANIEL BACON

Now last I talked to him, he told of you,

That, generous, he's given much to you,

These lands, these fine furrowed rows and slave

        hands,

He's given time in garden to wander,

And at the bare fruitless branch to ponder,

But now all of Jamestown's luckless needs plot[1],

For all the plans he has for us, for you,

No not e'en for barons will stop,

He has much children to burn his Blessing unto,

Much a country to invest his best crop,

Jamestown dogs are starving in the cage, James.

Will they be fed today?

James Drugger slowly stood to his feet.

JAMES DRUGGER

Know I've no faith in your feeding, Bacon.

I think these starving dogs, landless freemen,

Are a stomach aching without cess[2], that not

Even my plentiful fields would satisfy.

---

[1] indentured servants, after their terms expired, had
no open land to purchase, could only rent from richer
Barons.
[2] boundary, measure

Your men are sloths, drunks, sooner to fettle[1]

And shirk their lives than till a field or farm,

Sooner to embrothel than empeople,

Or murder than remake us Man,

Sooner to quaff[2] all a grog-bringer's beer

Than sober a wide wild wood to Culture.

They're of Jamestown's criminals composed, who

Only follow as they're led out jails.

Smooth skinned smooth tongued Nathaniel Bacon twisted under the tree laughing.

NATHANIEL BACON

Purl[3] like this did cut the head of our King.

Remember, Restoration returned the blow,

The counter-cuts beheaded their beheaders.

Remember well the end of Cromwell, [4]

Look, Jamestown's arms around your Garden.

Exit, Nathaniel Bacon.

JAMES DRUGGER
(*internal*)

Hypocritical mucker. Foul serpent.

I'd not loose an acre to his crawling ilk.

---

[1] to avoid labor with meaningless activity

[2] to drink copiously, with vigor

[3] bewitching speech

[4] Cromwell died in 1658, before being beheaded

He looked up at his tree again. Adam's hid behind a rig.

JAMES DRUGGER
(*internal*)

For her I still harbor a heart's feeling...

Marigold's a ship of safest passage.

But now I've pushed her too far off the bank,

That for fear of my bank,

Does Marigold have a heart of gold, or

Purse with a space vacuum'd to her effect?

To sentence upon the latter would be

To judge the former before its jury

Had its proper deliberations done,

Therefore judgement as yet be none,

Then my spurn was without an end, thus, thus...

Best to go to market and make amends.

Exit, James Drugger. Adam Thorngood reclined in the apple
tree. Picking his teeth with a thistle, he changed into Iostaf.

IOSTAF
(*winking; aside*)

This ends Act 1, with threads still to undone,

Unravels to Act 2, where

Time I'll realign to Tavern Deaf-John,

Where James' other to his lover sings song.

ACT 2

DEAF JOHN'S TAVERN – NIGHT

The space was thick with smoke and sound. Long banquet benches. Canakins cups mugs goblets tankards ran to their patrons jumped splashed to the drunk the drink. Shouts bellows rebellows and tall tales. There're rooms upstairs. Three old women there plucking. Boot-catcher boys rushed about like roaches offing all the boots from the centi-pieds of feet that wander they stowed them in pairs for pairs of pence and lost the other shoes dropped through the rotted floor.

The bartender Cursory the Turk hid in the corner his face covered in ash & wearing sackcloth drawers, mourning as Carousers revolved like days through the wild doggery. Iostaf's reclined in a candle sconce ey watched the scene.

IOSTAF

Smoke, sack, and a kiss suffuses bed-tricks,
James Joiner and 'servant' Ferdinando
Do bait, hook, and dress their inheritrix.

James Joiner, Marigold Mammon, and Ferdinando sat together at the far table. Their drained cups limp away in an

41

exhausted train. Ferdinando hailed Cursory the Turk over to their table, again, who wiped away his tears and put on big smiles.

FERDINANDO

Another round, aleberries for alebuddies!

CURSORY THE TURK

Aye, sirs!

Cursory ambled to it, scratching his sagging sides.

CURSORY THE TURK
(*to his anthro-morp'd cups*)

'Aye, sirs' – there's the tune my kind old cow died
On to. Oh Rachel, Rachel, wouldn't a woman live
Longer than a man, else a man is marred even
Ever after his marriage if love her he did. All this
I've inherited I immolate this 'I' in. Aye, inn...
Oh there's a job, that jabs a life all job,
And like old Job I'll stubborn'd say it so, so
All my life's complaint, so my life's my make.
Oi! You cups, to table with you! Double time,
Tankards, to it, to it, tankards! S'up! March!

The cups like tin soldiers march as man said. One salutes.
One tumbles off the table is cracked and never serves again.

CURSORY THE TURK

My cup runneth over!

JAMES JOINER
(*into Ferdinando's ear*)

Friend Ferdinando, our pence's all drained.

FERDINANDO

Marigold maid! My master James' generous!

Here's a man of wealth and charity mixed, see he

Who's wallet's deep as his heart! Aye, master?

We shirk neither charity nor the hoppedance[1]!

The communing drinks leap up onto the table and unashamed showed themselves they drank of them deep and left emptier than earlier.

JAMES JOINER
(*inebriated*)

Yes indeed my Marigold our deeds be

Pottle-deep[2], tis a hard trial upon us to mucker[3]…

Our gifts have no zippers but open drawers! No
        greed's

Beget'd for my widow'd pet, my lapping lap
        sparrow,

My arrow Mary, flame of burning heart, do douse
        me.

He kissed her. Marigold leaned back shocked.

---

[1] demon of the belly, associated with drunkenness

[2] roughly, a half-gallon's worth

[3] to hoard up money

MARIGOLD

My James in the deep-drink's as different

From his winter self as this November

Must be to summer in Spain.

FERDINANDO

His drinking deep

Tinder'd the flaming feelings of his heat,

As an alchemist burns by athanor[1],

Separates gold from materials poor, just so

His love for you's risen from dim to brim!

Marigold held back James' hand as it as it as it.

MARIGOLD MAMMON

My terms remain the same, you needs wed me.

FERDINANDO

We will, happily!

JAMES DRUGGER

I'll marry thee, Mary!

FERDINANDO

-gold

MARIGOLD

Well why didn't you wed me before, James?

FERDINANDO

Marry[2], Marigold, my master was afraid.

---

[1] an alchemist's furnace

[2] short for, 'by Mary', a mild oath, meaning truly

MARIGOLD

Is that true James? You were afraid of me?

JAMES JOINER

Aye, mam, as bald men fear the removal

Of their periwig, the false pale pate rev-ow!

-Ferdinando kicked him under the table.

JAMES JOINER

-Oh! Marigold! I'd marry you tonight,

I'd empty all purse, land… purse, to bypass

What portress guards the gates of your closed heart.

MARIGOLD

But just this morn you said I'd not see you,

As though your eyes were sore of me, and that

Was why you turned your back to me,

FERDINANDO

T'was castle

To the siege of your charm, looks, and beguile.

My master James' no master of love's ways.

Why, yesterday, while I was imprisoned

In the privy[1], through the fume-hole I heard

His rambles, for he talks as he ambles,

He said aloud what he'd kept under shroud:

'Twas far better be loved than love the beloved',

---

[1] an outhouse

Hearing such witch-heresy, and before

He'd burn himself on that anathema[1],

I rushed out to redeem, unbuttoned but bold!

Gluttons smokers cups growers servants sneakfeasts[2] all

the tavern were listening caught by Ferdinando.

FERDINANDO
(*as thespian*)

I made great claim and passioned pleas to all

Of those Marigold mammoth glitters and charms

That she most chaste possesses sans [3]slander!

Down I bellowed into the deep darkness

Of his blindness, 'Won't you rise from night,

　　　O mole?

Escape your grotto to her full sun light!'

With these words, cried as one in wilderness,

Prophesying my master to rightness,

Him I amazed, till both we stood stock-still

　　　in shock,

He for my words spoke unbuttoned,

I for my unhit hide,

Astounded my master did not whip me,

Or buffet a'blows, or enlock in stocks,

---

[1] imprecation, a curse
[2] one who steals another's dinner at table
[3] without

For my pander near pounced on usurp'tion!

But now I see my hubris was well spat,

For on his lap this maid is well well sat!

Applause! Cheers! Toasts-clack! Long live the King!

Embraces mugging. Fisticuffs smacking. A kiss upstairs a kiss downstairs James Joiner led Marigold by her guarding hand and Ferdinando brought them up a step. Up a stair. Hello! A sneakcup[1] (Iostaf) stole James' drink right out his hand! James bellowed shouted cursed raved laughed & made such a mad stir, ran about laughing looking for the thief shaking persons chasing a boot-catcher dancing with another red-handed one as to a clapp'd jig as three dark-hearted men puffing like dragons watch him from the corner,

Jenkin Price, William Watts, and Thomas Tooker.

JENKIN PRICE
(*quietly*)

William Watts, regard, James Drugger I see.

WILLIAM WATTS
(*quietly*)

Indeed,

And I'll tell our Nathaniel Bacon come.

It may be that in this wildness of drink,

---

[1] one who steals drinks at feasts

And we've never yet seen him ever drunk,

That wets may whet him keen to our wild cause,

So I'll bring this way our well-done Bacon.

Exit, William Watts.

THOMAS TOOKER

James! Stay, James, stay! How goes thy grow!?

JAMES JOINER

What grow??

FERDINANDO

It grows, goes, shows, mows, friend! Fare you well!

THOMAS TOOKER

Who's your black bastard, James?

JENKIN PRICE

Thane James on leaving should his leaves donate-

THOMAS TOOKER

-To the less fortunate-

JENKIN PRICE

-The landless free.

THOMAS TOOKER

Or the indentured servants, for a fee.

FERDINANDO

James does not his plots let lease to beggars,

Nor does he loose coins to

Clap-dishes, bibbers, hecklers, or pickthanks!

They booed him and threw buns stews and frightened cups.
Ferdinando led James and Marigold around in circles,
dodging the missiles but the crowd ringed around them. They
jostle them douse them pickpocket (nothing got). At the pitch
Iostaf shapeshifted into the shift of The Judge beat eir staff
on the floor like a gavel.

THE COURTROOM TAVERN –
AN ECLIPSE OCCURING[1]

The scene changes. The tavern moved their feast to the
arrangement of a stately courtroom rise, stand litigiously.

THE JUDGE

Please be pleased to be seated!

So they all did.

THE JUDGE
(*takes a deep swig of ale; smoking*)

Let the accuséd be brought to us forthwith!

A prisoner's led in, took the stand (an upturned apple box)
half-naked, young. A pear is punctured to the far wall by a
nail behind his head. Strangers throw darts at it. One hits.

PEAR NAILERS

Sebastian interruptus! Nail him on!

---

[1] for reasons of scarcity, taverns would double as law
courts, often for the prosecution of inebriation

THE JUDGE
(*gaveling his drained tankard*)

Order! Order now in this bar-and-Court!

You sir stand accused of public quaffing!

You've drunk drink excessively! Shame!

THE TAVERN

O' Shame!

THE JUDGE

What say you in your unpleasant defense?

THE TAVERN

What say you, sir!?

THE PRISONER
(*drunk*)

Hear, your Hinir! He whose-so hungovers should

Be hung till he's overs!

Applause. Nodding. Approval. Suddenly a wizened prospector from the new West (a few miles out) bursts in Court:

PROSPECTOR

This' not Jamestown!

This' but the dim-twin of true Form! Foller' me!

I've built the true townshape in the deep swamp!

Foller' me, up and out!

All rise the Tavern to follow him.

THE JUDGE

No, good people! Foller' not the madman!

His town's a two-walled shed on a wet hill!

Madman, all else ignorant are of your

James' town, don't you mind that?

PROSPECTOR

So's my left foot

Ignorant of my eye, but I don't mind!

Now a judge should know well the false and true,

And the sentence of his sentence gavels its period.

Jamestown, James' town, and that hidden Town

Of James, see, all three will go up in flames!

He hopped out the way he'd hopped in, on his left foot.
The Judge banged his tankard. Quiet in the Court of James.

THE JUDGE

Order! Let's return to our proceedings,

My balanced sentence I'll now say…

Prisoner, I charge you to stand on the skirts of

Our mother church for days three, with pottle hung

From thy adam's apple, thus decor'ing the Empty

And bottomless Soul of us when drink drains it.

Bang! his tankard. So he sentenced; all swigged in assent.
They carry out the drunk, puff pipes till all room's a'smoke.

Ferdinando pushes James and Marigold towards the door.
They slip under the smoke unseen until

Bang! The door.

Noise like warfare waged in the house. The clatter of a clamber couldn't contain into the tavern-court they came a drove of Diggers and a rabble of Ranters on court-floor they joust brawl to the busts.[1]

THE DIGGERS

(*loud big angry*)

The land is all! Anarch worker's worship!

THE RANTERS

(*faint small wimpy*)

We can, if it be our will, kiss and hug

M'ladies, and love our neighbor's wife as ourself...

A court of tennis they hurled mugs and buns and boys and coins and chamber-pots ping-pong slosh through the air. The Judge fled to his chambers (the john). The crowd spectated the bout, the Diggers winning (they threw clods).

Enter Edward Whalley[2], he grips James Joiner by the ear:

EDWARD WHALLEY

Once warred a banquet hall o'er a father,

In Whitehall the parliamentarians a

Tyrant did check, he who would in himself

---

[1] two 17th century English dissenting groups. The Commonwealth saw many such religious mobs emerge. They are here presented anachronistically

[2] a regicide (King-killer); supposedly he fled to the American colonies after the restoration of Charles II, whose father he had executed under Cromwell

A power dread over free people hold,

In such bellies Leviathan, a man,

A heavenly rebel, was raised to raze,

Who would not bend nor be swayed by power

In appearance only omnipotent,

Mortal Cromwell deific King defied,

And rolled the fields of England like red waves

Of flames by the machinery of mob,

King was caught and de-necked[1], hebetate[2], held

By holy hair, the King's fading eyes did gaze

Down on the crowd, his children they were,

By them his gentle head had hat'd a crown,

To lead them for his time, a king his reign,

Did as the rain his blessings let fall,

Until the drought, his dread sway, dries all out,

The Blessing broke, the People spoke, 'Off with…'

Then the executioner's hand he wore

For them on his lifted-up head, as

His lips mimed still his prayer for the dead,

Until the sovereign Voice himself was dead.

---

[1] King Charles I was beheaded in 1649 by the Parliament which would then form the British Commonwealth
[2] blunted; dull; lifeless

The battle rages the Ranters form a fort of tables chairs cups
in the corner and were there besieged by the Diggers.

EDWARD WHALLEY

What were his trickling thoughts when his apple

Was from hand to basket let go to Fall?

JAMES JOINER

Marry, he thought, 'hiccius doccius,

The King's become harlequin, he's juggled.'

EDWARD WHALEY

Nay, James, his were ticks of clocking Kronos:

All of my children I should have eaten.

Whaley slipped out into the cold.

The Diggers and Ranters their battle brought them cross the
floor out the door over snow into the Atlantic to sink.

Eclipse. John Smith and his column of ragged troops march
in[1]. They carry a man above their heads a needle pierced
his tongue sentenced to starve to death for stealing bits of
bread when starving to death. They tied him to a lone tree.

Pocahauntus[2] is led on by rope weeping tears for a trailwalk.

---

[1] John Smith, an English soldier and explorer, led the
colony of Jamestown between 1608 and 1609

[2] 'Pocahontas' was a princess of the Powhatan people
until being held for ransom by Jamestown colonists

Smith's troops marched her around 13 times. Exiting, they
fire their muskets at the black moon, and all faded in dark.

Enter, Larkin White dancing from the famines of Jamestown.

LARKIN WHITE
(on a gallows; noosed)

O' a wife's such a delectable dish,

She's quieter cooked than you'd ever wish,

If you've the famine, and you can't get by,

Then turn your wife into mutton mince pie!

Lop all the limbs, chop up both the eyes,

Boil down bones, forget me not to powder' nose,

Dig out what root and herb can be got,

Fennel femur a pinch of toes a pair of parsley,

Salsify, mint, tongue, and the strings of muscle,

A rooty leg a long arm a lake's bulrush stalk,

All go into the pot!

When my cooking was caught,

Before the noose went taut,

I said this, it was true,

Have I done wrong?

Have I done wrong?

---

in 1613; she was converted to Christianity during this
time.

I dreamt I was eating my shoe,

I woke in the night with a terrible fright,

To see that meal was my wife, Sue.[1]

Snap. He's hanged to death. Virginians, thick as an ancient wood, ran through the tavern. Hear. Stampede! They pull up floorboards the black mud there. They dig up all the pyrite they can find and hock it. They turn into goldust their widows remarry the next day, rings of fool's gold on their fingers.[2]

James Joiner, Ferdinando, Marigold, in a daze rushed for the door – it opened.

DEAF JOHN'S TAVERN – EVENING

In the doorway, Werowance, a Native, three hunted wolf's heads hang from his belt. All watched the Amerikan.

He walked to the bar. He exchanged the wolf's heads with Cursory the Turk for a receipt for two milkcows to pasture.

He drank a shot of aleberry.

He turned to face them.

---

[1] recorded in journals by John Smith

[2] Jamestown was founded for gold extraction; this was changed to tobacco planting, as smoking was found to attenuate the feeling of false gold

WEROWANCE[1]

In the beginning, there was no thing but water. And
this water was as nothing but itself, and someway,
no man will know the why, from the water there
arose a mist, which was the sky, the very breath of
Kokomaht, the Creator. Bodiless, nameless,
motionless, bodied, named, motioning, he became a
being two – his twin was on his back, was his back,
until a split. The first of the two rose up through the
fathoms, his eyes closed, above the waves, he rose,
and himself he named Kokomaht, the good god, for
that was the memory he wanted. But his twin was
still below, and shouted up, 'Brother, how did you
rise?' and Kokomaht, guileful, simply said, open
your eyes. The twin opened his eyes, and he rose
and was struck blind by the full fathomed way up –
Kokomaht named him Bakotahl, Blind One. Then
Kokomaht did make the heavens and the earth, and
all things he formed, while Bakotahl, feeling with
his hands everything his twin made, also made the
same, but his were mud pies, without life, beauty,

---

[1] Werowance's story is adapted from a Yuma Tribe
story recorded by Natalie Curtis, and edited by
Richard Erdoes, and Alfonso Ortiz

his creations were clumsy. Bakotahl was sad, he sank beneath the earth to sleep. Then Kokomaht began to die, by his own will this was,for he knew how to die, to die was to make more room for his children, so to them all he called, and they came, all men. But the White Man would not come, but stayed in the West, weeping for himself, his washed-out skin, and the walls of his own greed which he did built around himself. Kokomaht pitied his sons, the White Man, so he sent him two sticks, tied in the shape of a cross, for him to lie on, and this became a mighty horse, the first horse. The White Man was happy, but still he did not visit his Creator, so as justice, no matter where the White Man rode his Horse, his seat would soon change, and he'd see it was again a cross he lay on. So the White Man will always suffer. For he will not get off it. For that cross on which he lies lasts not long before a change of it he will demand. But he can never really change it. Not until from off it he come to walk with his brothers, Red Man and others. Kokomaht's last words were, 'Learn How to Die'. And his body was burned the first of the funeral pyres. But his soul still lives, a wild spirit, which

moves everywhere, and can be seen in the wind that
drives Fall leaves before us, or Spring seeds, or our
black hair. When the house of Kokomaht was
brought down, for this house had to follow him, a
great well flowed from the earth, and there came the
lakes and the rivers, filled with creatures strange,
the clumsy creations of Bakotahl, the Blind One,
and these were the fish and all the water creatures,
for Kokomaht had made no water creatures. When
Bakotahl wakes, and remembers his changed twin,
and the tricks that were played on him, and his bad
creations, he throws a temper tantrum, and from
that comes all earthquakes and pestilence, so from
all good things came Kokomaht, all evil, from
Bakotahl, who doesn't really mean to, this is how
all things were, are, will be. But Wise Man
remembers, and says to remind, these two twins
Were once One.

Quiet. Big boots banging to the door. It opens: Nathaniel
Bacon, black. His eyes, they narrow on the Indian. William
Watts, Jenkin Price, and Thomas Tooker, his lackeys, armed
with knives, surrounded Werowance and sat him down.

The native Amerikan, he allowed them to touch him.

NATHANIEL BACON

I heard a nitchie[1] had caught all your ears.

Now you'll listen to him…

From the tavern floor a rumbling like an earthquake. The tavern shook. Nuncle[2] SAHM sleeps under the tavern stirred almost to rousing he quaked tossed turned groaned for all Jamestown to hear:

NUNCLE SAHM
(*dreaming*)

Grow Tobacco! Growww Tobaccooo!

NATHANIEL BACON

Here lies asleep in our country's cellarage[3]

A Dreng[4] of force and form, great in his goal,

Yet mickle[5] more doth he sloth in gaol[6],

Dreaming on his fall, weeping for his wake,

Regrowing his limbs great, his bearded gorge,

His kynemark[7], and his stones of offspring,

For dungen[8] he fell into this dungeon rest,

---

[1] this rude and derogatory slur comes from an Ojibwe word for 'friend'

[2] archaic, meaning 'Uncle'

[3] the storeroom of a cellar

[4] derived from an Old English term for Warrior

[5] very much

[6] a jail

[7] a cross shaped birthmark

[8] beaten; execrated

Cast out from the rest of old ironsides[1], and

Shot over endless Atlantic, as if

From a keep-besieging catapult, cast out,

A scorching meteor, cast out, cratering

The New World, an early grave, on this spot,

This very mark, was he marred to rest, sleep,

And low forever lie, unless himself

He shall remember again to giant,

Then as dread lord, wrathful he will re-rise,

And walk in long strides his joyful blue eyes

His far leagues upon this earth's early green,

This infant land, this new world, this bounty

For all brothers of God, so I've seen when

Here I've smoked the strong jimsonweed[2]

Open'd my ears am to all the word of he,

These lobes to tavern floor I've placed, and heard

As through a door these things to have the fits

Of Visions fitted to my mind, as now,

Now... yes, I hear something on our horizon,

I auger, that we grow from coast to coast,

With the felling of trees and the laying

---

[1] apparently the giant, SAHM, is an exile from
England known as 'old ironsides'

[2] also known as the devil's snare, a poisonous
flowering plant; may be smoked for harrowing
hallucinogenic effect

Of metal in long veins to mark the course

Of his body, and us his blood, do race

'Cross the corpus 'round, knitting the body,

From us bodies a Body... I see

That we seed our fruits, multiply a nation,

Burgeon[1] a Blessing, and bind to a deal,

Us most, what an US, of Nuncle SAHM's host!

The Tavern, of whites, blacks, bewitched by the ear Bacon thro' their heady midst as he spoke shaking their hands & their lobes.

NATHANIEL BACON

These, and yet more great futures I've seen,

When I've smoked the foretelling jimsonweed.

O' brothers, o' my brothers, I remember,

I remember how we, arm in arm to arms,

The Dutch dogs' invasions[2] repelled

By force of brotherhood and Providence

Divine, when Egyptian hurricanes, and

The plagues of hailstorms for full forty days,

Sent them fleeing into the waving sea,

---

[1] to shoot forth a bud, as a flower from a wooden staff

[2] On August 27th, 1667, a hurricane struck the Jamestown colony, destroying their fort at Old Point Comfort, yet simultaneously driving off the Dutch fleet raiding along their coast

For we are Israelites a colony,

I choose us a chosen people,

All has been to defend

Our Mankin Slumberer, our Giant Man,

Our benevolent father, our Nuncle SAHM.

Ghostly as a flag (of many colors) winked behind him. The
crowd the crowd democrat'd him clapping clapping.

NATHANIEL BACON
(*gripping Werowance by his hair*)

And yet, and yet, and yet our Governor,

Our purpose and power to him entrusted,

Governor William Berkeley[1], has risked

Our Giant Dreamer's very life, which is the

Destiny manifesting in young hearts

To grow, this has stalled, for *what* has dread drem[2]

Been shaken? For this savage I hold up

By his hair here, this thing of skin hellish,

Red Edom man, hardly man at all he

Our Governor guards, he

Who's bewitched by their rattling staffs of snakes

Or chants of tongue that march to devil's drum,

Enthralled under their persuasions, Berkeley's

---

[1] aristocratic governor of Virginia between 1641-
1652, 1660-1677
[2] dream

Locked away the virgin lands from our hands[1],

Which we'd take not for overleaping ambition,

But for our families to feed, for freedom

For our families to grow, for growth of us

Of the soils of our pioneering husbandry,

This only we ask, no more, no more noble

Request could we bring before him our King-

Like Governor… And yet it is denied,

For whom is this denied?

Bacon's lackeys now picked up Werowance and held him up
sprawled before the crowd. They shave his hair off his head.

NATHANIEL BACON

We uplift the loathsome thing above you,

This is us Sathanas[2], imago Sathanus,

The fallen one, light bringer within us,

Within our very midst… an open door is

The frontiers of our homes, he's squatting there,

Grinning over his wicked goals, envies,

Lusts, plans his own invasion par Phillip[3]

---

[1] Agricultural expansion had been forbidden by the
Governor for fear of Native reprisal. King Phillip's
War in New England was still being waged at this
time, and served as the stern warning of example
[2] the devil
[3] King Phillip, Metacomet, was sachem (leader) to
the Wampanoag people until his death on August
12th, 1676

To murder our children, our wives, steal our land,

So this I now do say:

We'll clip these growsome weeds,

Trample, burn, their teepees,

As a sink we'll drain our land of our filth,

Idleness, and all unclean savagery,

This is my promise to you my people,

Persons New World'd, each man here

Will be to himself and his own heart free,

Master of his own house, tiller of his field,

New Man Amerikan!

Applause. Shaved Werowance was thrown out the door down into snow. James Joiner rushed to shake Bacon's hand.

JAMES JOINER

Oh sir, hear me just to say that your words

Have me so inspired, that henceforth, I and what's

  mine's

With you.

NATHANIEL BACON

I'm pleased your mind I've changed, now you're

Brother to me, forever un-estranged.

I will call on you soon.

Exit, Bacon and his lackeys. The drunks stumble homeward. Ferdinando and Marigold met James Joiner at the door.

FERDINANDO

What did you say to him?

JAMES JOINER

That his tale was

Curled an oracle – spoken of truth and times

To come. I told him that to him James's joined!

FERDINANDO

James, my master, this man is no friend to us,

His curling's a cruelness, I know his type,

This common kind I've seen from birth. Listen:

Before you bought me, when I was taken

From my homeland, scores of Spanish slavers

This black Bacon's butchering aspect wore,

He loves not country, but the rush of ruling,

He fears not freedom, but feeling power,

He strips all backs not his with whips of tongs, and

With silver tongues, sways he all to slavery.

James Joiner took Marigold by the hand, kissed her, and led
them out into the winter evening.

JAMES JOINER

Now my slave should silent as silence be,

And shall not lean on the affairs of his betters.

This Bacon will bring about a Roundhead's[1]

Revolution, for whites, and blacks, and women.

Fall in line, master'll unlink all fetters.

FERDINANDO

(*outraged*)

My master's line's link is lacking in length,

My master's mask lacks the able strength to mask

The Cain-must of his intoxication,

My mule master mud is led by his horns[2],

Horned not for what we'd hound, but for a man,

This Bacon Devil that's caught you, cleft you,

And chapped his churl.

JAMES JOINER

You go beyond your bound-

FERDINANDO

-Let Bacon sizzle on his plan, and leave you

From out the palm of his hand, the sway seams

You less a White master, more a blanched slave.

JAMES JOINER

(*outraged*)

Thou knave!

FERDINANDO

I mean you to save!

---

[1] supporters of the Parliament of England during the
English Civil War, they fought against King Charles I
[2] by tradition, horns were the symbol of the cuckold

JAMES JOINER

> I whip for this.

FERDINANDO
(shaking his hand stiffly; bowing)

I thank you for your kind services, master sir,

But as we've lined as far as our garment may run,

I'll unjacket myself, out your doublet,

For that benefit's all ebbed, the terms end,

I shake hands', betters, bow, untie, and go!

Exit, angrily,

JAMES JOINER

Ferdinando!

MARIGOLD

Your servant's given much leeway of leering

On you, my love.

JAMES JOINER

> Yes, yes, I will punish

Him then. Remain here my Marigold till

I return, and I'll have brought some fine ring

To wed you with…

Exit, James Joiner.

Marigold gads about Jamestown under the rising moon the soon snowing night. Close the curtains two.

ACT 3

THE INDIAN WOODS – MIDNIGHT

Ferdinando gads alone among avenue trees musing, musing.

He sees a column of black men in chains wander through towards town their chains clink, clink towards Jamestown.

FERDINANDO

A mirror's a man, so I've seen them so,

Under black aspect of a whipman's eye,

When his slave fallen by the sun does spy,

Black and black does their burnings match, one,

For water and shade, other, for pleasure,

Yet this parity permits an easy

Exchange, a rage for rage, whereby I heard

Myself making the high shouting crack of

The whip that's black, until of the dust my

Master was the slave, so

I was drawn, from the whip, to wield my Word

On my mirrors, meeting my twins and

Seizing my twins and swapping place like the

Station, so rising my station to top

Myself over the time,

Flee the foolery of Time.

He enters a grove. He kneels over a grey pool of water.

FERDINANDO

James Joiner on the Blackpool dock I thought

My ablest reflection so joined he was

To that my mind's meaning,

'What, James, is wealth but the means of freedom,

What freedom but permission to poetry,

What poetry but Word bridging an I within?'

In the pool, an old man with white hair white beard his finger
pointing out. Ferdinando ruptures the water with his hand.

FERDINANDO

These early brands on hued skin will burn

In letterings that by tropes of history

Will write in something most evil, a cist,

A 'cism, into which all will fall in chains,

Burn begins in us brands.

He stands up.

FERDINANDO

I'll permit that us on none of this me,

Au revoir, James, my mirror shattered, my

Time's turned on me that which made me me,

Oh then there's twin in the times indeed, I

Wanting all, will sink this eye in Dismal Swamp,

Where some of my family's fled to, and there

My reflections muddy may at last stop,

And stop.

Exit, Ferdinando.

THE MARKET– THE NEXT MORNING

Bustlers. Costermongers. Tobacco hawkers. Marigold goes
through the market. Jamestown men bow to her as she passes
over them as they tip their hats lay down their coats. Adam
Thorngood hails Marigold as she passes his stall of pots.

ADAM THORNGOOD

Maid Marigold! Let snow fall on Marigold!

MARIGOLD MAMMON

Adam Thorngood! Today I would rename,

'Very good', it's been made so by my James,

For he's been freed from his in-fettered cave,

And walks hand in my hand in brightest day,

O' joy, Adam! O' beautiful country!

How long I've longed for our love to be born,

Now is brought to birth my 'he will laugh'[1], for

---

[1] the literal meaning of the name, 'Isaac'

In love I laugh, feeling our youth, which laughs

At age's approach and removes death remote.

ADAM THORNGOOD

Maid Marigold! Let snow fall on Marigold!

Let the reminders of winter regress,

Chill, cold and cool the inflaméd amper[1]

That swells thy heart to believe a bantling[2]

Love from pre-broken promise comes.

Widow, this child's not even a chrisom,

Who dies just after his baptism, not even

As living as that is this James the second,

King of mischief.

Enter, James Drugger.

ADAM THORNGOOD

Here comes his shadow, or

The casting self-thereof.

MARIGOLD

Adam, why do you try to take my joy?

ADAM THORNGOOD
(imitating owl call)

Who-cooks-for-you, who-cooks-for-you-all!

Exit, Adam. Enter, James Drugger.

---

[1] a tumor; a defect
[2] an infant, illegitimate

JAMES DRUGGER

Marigold, I do beg of your pardon,

I don't toy with your heart, but broken's mine,

If you could see, frost's formed on reddest parts.

Where's most in tender, most in loving, there

Our worst wounds much en-scar, so hearts harden

Of hearts, and our love by love loses loving,

Thus we do save ourselves from what would save.

MARIGOLD

James, I know, your servant's already

This nature explained, that our wounds shared

In wounding of each our other,

Yet just as much a match is this,

This nurture, that by this us, repairs our nature,

Histories of hurt are in hands bandaged.

She kissed him. He pulled away.

JAMES DRUGGER

My servant? My servant?? Who that I own

Would to my mistress divulge his master's heart?

MARIGOLD

James, you know who, you were with him yourself

When he returned your heart to me again.

JAMES DRUGGER

What is this fib, some new strategy?

What servant base turns heart of mastery?

73

MARIGOLD

Ferdinando…

JAMES DRUGGER

No, I own no such man.

MARIGOLD

Then what is he to you? What do you gain

By *your* fib? If Ferdinando is free,

Then his talk to soften me was by fee,

And almost ushered me with you to bed

As quick as sheets were an honest altar,

But I'd wear my penance in white to church

Before we'd ever marry there, as you claimed.[1]

JAMES DRUGGER

This trick is no way to make me marry.

I said no such thing.

MARIGOLD

Yes you-

JAMES DRUGGER

-When?

MARIGOLD

Last night.

---

[1] This is a reference to the Jamestown practice of forcing a couple to wear white sheets and carry white wands in church, during services, as penance for fornication, adultery, and other offences of the bed

74

JAMES DRUGGER

No, I said no such thing.

MARIGOLD

You were drunk…

JAMES DRUGGER

Liar, bawd, and drunk she charges on me!

I am dull dry sober and I say I've

Said no such things, nor made marriage promises,

Nor is my heart wheeled by a slave on his loom,

Nor will I be deceived by the lace tricks

Of an opportunist inheritrix

As inconstant as the moon.

Marigold held her chest, wounded.

Enter, John Pot, buyer of James Joiner and Ferdinando, who waddled up to James Drugger, bumped him with his stall that he wore like a skirt.

JAMES DRUGGER

Clumsy wide jag[1]! Mind your lobby boat.

JOHN POT

James!

My slow slave, still biting for a whipping?

You idle in market when to my plantation

You must report.

---

[1] drunkard

MARIGOLD

Are you not James? Has some dark shadow you

Yourself replaced? And in your place put this,

This man of the frost and icy regard?

Have old fears marred morbose[1] your heart?

Or by that wicked Bacon, who's bewitched

You away from me?

JAMES DRUGGER
(*to John Pot*)

You will wait a moment won't you, want-wit?

(*to Marigold*)

I spoke with Nathaniel Bacon and found

Him no more than a tinder of scarefire[2],

I'm not heart-turned by likes of him either.

(*to John Pot*)

Your drunken shab's run its puddering course.

Shove off, thou fattest boat.

James shoved John Pot and tipped him over and the stall he
wore propped him and he rolled about like a strange wheel.

JOHN POT

Help! Help! Murder by slave! Servant's uprising!

---

[1] diseased

[2] one who alarms fire under false pretenses, usually
for the burglary of unwatched goods

MARIGOLD

(*striking him*)

James! You deceiver!

JAMES DRUGGER

I shouldn't have looked

For you, widow Marigold. No, let this

Be our final dissunder-

MARIGOLD MAMMON

-So be it so!

Exit, her. Enter, three armed guardsmen.

GUARDSMAN

Are you James Drugger?

JAMES DRUGGER

I'm certain of that, yes.

GUARDSMAN

The Governor, William Berkeley, wishes

To see you, sir.

JAMES DRUGGER

Then lead me to him, sirs.

Exit, James. John Pot rolls about.

GOVERNOR BERKELY'S MANSION – MORNING

James Drugger was let in, left there to find his way within.

The mansion, dark and quiet and rich. He wandered, rooms,

libraries, bedrooms, parlors, burning fireplaces, all empty of
Berkeley. He enters what appears to be a study at the top.

JAMES DRUGGER

If a man be nowhere, he may appear
Anywhere, and so I'll sit me now here.

A comfortable, warm armchair. There was a portrait of
Berkley – a pale man with billowing wig baggy black eyes
clasping his white gloved hands tight together – on the wall.

Berkeley wore a wide white hat which shaded his face so that
the face could not be seen. James found this same white hat
propped on a desk before him; James picked it up and was
surprised to find the Governor sat under it staring up at him.

GOVERNOR BERKLEY

Would you kindly replace my wall white hat?
James Drugger apologized & carefully set the hat back down
on the Governor's head. From under the hat:

GOVERNOR BERKLEY

James Drugger, planter rich in leaf and land,
Do you love your king? I love my king much,
Enough, too much. I'm caught in quite the puzzle,
I've promised, promoted, this young man,

This young, young one, who's like, he's like,

> offspring,

This Bacon, Nathaniel, Nathan Bacon.

He stood up on his chair. He wasn't very tall but taller than
James by the chair. He raised his arms his white hat wider.

GOVERNOR BERKLEY

Like some sovereign Zeus shook I hoary locks,

Showers gold fell from me to glamor he,

As sun does dew the lawn to shine in rays,

And reflect lights of power I on him rained,

My scepter I son'd from my hand

To his, and said to him, down power's glance,

'Bacon be an Amerikan of peace,

Trample not on thy neighbor the Indian,

We must measure on scales their good and bad,

From savages, part the reformable clay,

The latter we do form, on potter's wheel,

And burn in kiln of King's catholic faith

To shape of Man reformed, to toil our lands,

By water dewing from their brows'.

He stood up on the desk and leaned over the still seated
James under the great shadow of his boatbig white hat.

GOVERNOR BERKELY

Exploit, exploit, exploit, expedition

This New World, extract mineral, expand

Our manufactures of man. Look, I hold

Out to you, the silkworm on its sprig[1], see,

Gentle turnings, reelings of slender thread,

By such a slight string we'd hook the favor

Of our King, this is the clew[2] to the globe,

As the line is to yarn, I tell ye,

These low laboring insects princes endress,

Drape all the queens in canary yellows,

Or curtain incesting royalty's bowers,

All the trappings of color, that by the

Senses entrap the seer's envy, and

Sleight the might of Kings, begin in worm's bolg[3]

All these digesting things.

But if worm makes the power, and power

The man, then the grower of this the worm

Spins a wider wheel indeed, I'd have my

Amerikan Indians be spinners such

As these, I revolving them,

Thus the Powers to please, empowers me

To do what I please.

---

[1] Governor Berkley had introduced the silkworm to
Virginia as a means to diversify the tobacco economy
[2] ball of yarn
[3] stomach

Dizzy, he turned, looked out his window, bumped his hat brim on the glass like a metronome, keeping some thought of the times. He stops but keeps his back turned.

GOVERNOR BERKLEY

Bacon, my son, son-ish, took some men down

To the river Roanoke, where the

Friendly Occaneechees's had held a number

Of the Susquehannahs, our enemies,

Captive prisoners, upon the mercy of us.

Bacon beckon'd his men to shoot, all fell

Dead our enemies. Bacon beckon'd yet

Again, fire, and all them our allies fell

Under his fire, a fire indiscriminate…

Bacon, all Indian he would exterminate.[1]

Good then bad would burn both in the kiln,

The good would be the dead.

Pause.

JAMES DRUGGER

If I may say so sir this Bacon has

Approached me with tender offers to join

Him in his Mission, to un-let my land

---

[1] the indiscriminate massacre occurred in May, 1676, as part of an illegal, racial crusade led by Nathaniel Bacon

To the hands of his brigands, prisoners,

And beggars.[1] This also I've heard, that our

Many taverns he visits sly on the night,

To ply the ears of the nicotine'd hearts

Toward Mission, which I think the veils for

His ambition, built on pretense to goals

Of the planting, the growing, the budding

Of a new Nation, separate from our

Honorable England-Albion[2].

Of course, him I refused. I trust not his

Anti-Indian talk, and think it but

The mask for this darker part, meaner plot,

That he resents the rich I do suspect-

> GOVERNOR BERKELY
> (*his head in pain*)

-Ah! Aaahhh!

A servant knocked on the door and brought in three books on a platter: A grammar book a botanist's journal and a romance. Berkley tore their pages stomped on them sweated. Satisfied, tired, the Governor sat down in his chair, allowing his hat brim to prop up his head. James Drugger stared...

---

[1] at that time in history, as much as 10,000 acres of Virginia land were in the gloves of 30 wealthy barons persons

[2] mythic giant of Old England

GOVERNOR BERKLEY

(*from under the hat*)

When the moment's ripe, I can call on you?

JAMES DRUGGER

…Marry, I and what's mine is with you, sir.

GOVERNOR BERKLEY

Go then, wait on thy Sower's call.

JAMES DRUGGER

Farewell.

Exit, James Drugger.

GOVERNOR BERKLEY

Enter, guardsman. What do you call yourself?

Enter, Guardsman.

GUARDSMAN

I, sir?

GOVERNOR BERKLEY

Yes, so.

GUARDSMAN

'I', sir.

GOVERNOR BERKLEY

Yes, so.

Pause.

GOVERNOR BERKLEY

Well, man?

GUARDSMAN

Oh, yes, I am sir thank you sir. How're you?

GOVERNOR BERKLEY

Well! Well! What do you call yourself,

guardsman!?

GUARDSMAN

Well I call myself 'I' sir, as I said, sir.

GOVERNOR BERKLEY

Your name, your name! What is your name??

GUARDSMAN

(*puzzled*)

Oh! Name, sir? Name… hmm, well I've always

gone

by 'I'. Well, I don't think they've given no other.

GOVERNOR BERKLEY

What in the devil do you mean by 'they'?

Does 'I' mean its parents by this 'they', 'I'?

GUARDSMAN

You what, sir?

GOVERNOR BERKLEY

Oh devil, oh devil…

GUARDSMAN

Deviled eggs, sir?

GOVERNOR BERKLEY

No-bloody-dam-dev-you-egg-grumble-egg-

He knocked over all his things on his desk with his hat.

GOVERNOR BERKLEY

(*picking them up*)

'I'… 'I' come, come. Pick up these things.

GUARDSMAN

Yes, you are sir.

GOVERNOR BERKLEY

Filthy 'I'! A pox on the boggler!

GUARDSMAN

Don't be harsh

On yourself sir, see now, I will help you with the

spilled knickknacks and desk shoons[1]. 'Ard'pon

Your caring of me, tis a good master that cares

For his servants so well sir, aye, asking after

Their health, their names, their parentage

an'all that.

Aye, especially for one without a name as I,

sir, aye.

GOVERNOR BERKLEY

I don't care what your name is anymore!

Now listen you pocks puddle, ditch in road,

Pebble in shoe, a'blotch in map-

GUARDSMAN

-beam in eye?

---

[1] shoes

Berkely roars like a warrior aged beyond his arm.

GOVERNOR BERKLEY
(*chasing the guardsman around*)

I!? I!? I have an order for you, 'I'!

I order 'I' to spy with its eyes on

James Drugger! And I expect 'I' to keep

All its eyes will eye him!

Berkely by his hat bumps the Guardsman onto the ground.

GOVERNOR BERKLEY

Do *you* understand?

GUARDSMAN
(*standing up*)

I overstands sir.

GOVERNOR BERKLEY

Aye, there's my good spy, roll to it, my eyes.

GUARDSMAN

Aye aye!

(*winking; aside*)

Power resents a caught in Comedy!

Exit, Guardsman, who was actually Iostaf in disguise.

THE CROSSROAD – AFTERNOON

Iostaf on the road to James Drugger's plantation. Enter, James Joiner, still out looking for his friend Ferdinando.

IOSTAF

Hello! A good afternoon to James J!

JAMES JOINER

Oh, hello. Do I know thee, friend?

IOSTAF

As friend!

But know that 'I' brings a word from Bacon,

James… Drugger, he'd see you on your plantation!

JAMES JOINER

Oh! Who's plantation?

IOSTAF

Yours.

JAMES JOINER

Mine?

IOSTAF

Thine.

JAMES JOINER

Oh,

I -

IOSTAF

- Well, will you wend your way?

JAMES JOINER

Well, well I'll

Wend!

Confidently James Joiner walked in the wrong direction.

IOSTAF

James…

JAMES JOINER

Yes?

IOSTAF

Won't you go there now?

JAMES JOINER

Going!

He turned his direction & strutted in the wrong direction.

IOSTAF

James…

JAMES JOINER
(*improvs; plucks a fern; turns*)

I was simply admiring these New World ferns, sir!

Fine green frills! I'll make a fan of them to

Fan my mistress in heat, or let her shade

Her gaze behind their fingers, like lady

In coquetry, for love's game's a kind of croquet!

Now he was going the right way for the Dismal Swamp, but the wrong way for James Drugger's plantation.

IOSTAF

(*linking to him arm in arm*)

Sir James, allow me to steer you the way

To your plantation and lands rich in leaf!

For I've found short cuts there, and would bend

  your

Ear to if you'd let me lead and conduct!

JAMES JOINER

(*fanning himself with his fern*)

I will allow that, sudden friend – ear on.

Iostaf is taking James to his twin's plantation, where he'll
meet the black in heart Bacon & his snouted men and curling
tales of wicked Indians that make murder on the forest trails.

IOSTAF

(*aside*)

Exactly!

Now as us 'I' does to plantation go,

In the duration will show Ferdinando,

For he'll stumble on the maid Marigold,

Whose beauty's so bright, ll'bring heat to his cold!

Like this play, that weds new to that is old!

Exit, Iostaf.

THE GREAT DISMAL SWAMP, ON A
MAROON COLONY[1] – SUNSET

An island in a swamp. A few bungalows shacks and a gloomy

elderly donkey there. A raised log drawbridge there. Look

here's Ferdinando lounged in his hammock smoking. away

Dismal indeed! His family in the shack are sizzling an otter

on a skillet. Blue smoke rising.

Enter, Marigold filthy and abundant in swamp things.

MARIGOLD

Ferdinando!

FERDINANDO

Hey-o! Who's there!?

MARIGOLD

Marigold!

FERDINANDO

Marigold who!?

MARIGOLD

Why, Marigold Mammon!

Ferdinando! Lower your drawbridge!

FERDINANDO
(*glancing; nonchalant; eyes closed*)

I'd rather remain hammocked, rigged on my rig,

---

[1] Since the beginning of American slavery, the
Great Dismal Swamp served as a foreboding and so
well-hidden sanctuary for runaways & refugees

Marigold threw pebbles like a trebuchet which convinced Ferdinando to welcome in the invader. She crossed the skinny log bridge as he on hammock on high puffed smoke.

FERDINANDO

I surrender, conquering hero-ess.

Ferdinando's mother came out of a tent with a bowl of cooked otter which she gave to Marigold then returned in.

FERDINANDO

Why are you not with my diswitted James?

And why do you smell and seem such a swamp?

MARIGOLD

Your James has led me into the swamp maze.

I don't know what's right and what's left, what's

> up,

What's down, who's who, or where's who or, or

> who

Any one should be.

He offered her a smoke. She took a puff sending a prac-ticed ring of smoke sailing through the air.

MARIGOLD

> I wandered for far thoughts…

I lost myself, lost in this swamp, to knees

Up in such mire and muck, in the concerns

Of lizard's tail and mistflower, jumpseed,

And wild squaw-root, hognose snakes seemed grass

So together they congregated there,

Waving thick under the green docks of duckweed,

I found what path I could, there was little

Light under the canopy, following trails

Of fairy fire, untimely lighting for me

Their delusive shine, so that which I saw, lanterns

Of familied households, misled me further in

Bog, the lights went out, darkness,

Afraid, I stood in the pools of darkness,

A step I'd there misplace and place of swamp

I would usurp, Marigold ghost of ponk[1], witch of

The Great Dismal, the Great Widow, dissed by

A planter James, whose name I'd wail into

The ears of lost lovers that in my slough

Would by their recur-confusions wander,

And by chance the castaway may my visage

Spy, where in the green water the image lay,

'Here haunts the lovers lost' those bubbles

Would spell, when from the dead lips my airs

Would leak up to tell, to warn, all youths or

Youths in hearts, 'To love's to lose, sooner or later.'

Such were my auguries when in the dark pools

---

[1] a nocturnal spirit

I stood stockstill, afraid to chance a step,

But then, of an instant, I remembered me

A tobacco baron, just as much's he, who

Always carries a pouch of her rich leaf

And a tinder to light embers in her pipe,

Let there be, light I struck from the stone,

The sparks I caught, borne, nurtured on a

Handful of tobacco, I stacked high in

The bowl, a torch, by this, balanced me on airy

Tree roots which twist and turn above the swamp

Like words in dreams of depth past calls of strange:

Salamanders, sirens, ancient crocodile,

Avoiding their voices yet their appearance

Seemed to accumulate, I accreting bog

From stench below and reaching moss above,

Which touched then clutched my hair like rude

       suitors,

As though this world were naught but another man,

And I were naught but another woman

Under a man, under eyes that did clutch

Along the troping lines of twisting roots

An educating way, what may lead me out,

And when I became a thing swamp, haggy ponk,

Witch of her own wandering mis-following,

Hair of nettles and knotweed and sedge face

And skin of slime and cheek of corruption,

All my pores greening with inhumid growth…

Only then I got out, to stand before you, gross.

FERDINANDO

Indeed you are quite frightening, swamp-ponk.

MARIGOLD

So monster must I've always seemed to James!

Who stomached bravely my fulsome[1] aspect,

Who out of pity for my slavery,

Did consent to kiss me, yet no sooner

The taste of me acquired than he did spat

Me out like a sup lukewarm – swamp water!

FERDINANDO

Then slithered you back to your marshy bower.

MARIGOLD

Rejected, banished, in part for that Bacon,

By whom James would advance his station,

That thirst in-him in-parched, he lapped after

Power as for water, and shed all who

Would shed their blood would it yet quench his
        thirst,

He was most eager to disavow you too,

Pricked by shame for his servant's sway on him.

---

[1] offensive; excessive; ugly

94

His hurts hounded me here,

To sway listless by his leftover.

FERDINADO

To besiege my hammocking keep of pipe's peace.

MARIGOLD

I don't know what to do.

I'd always thought,

'I may never be free,

Till he enthrall me.'[1]

But in the dark pools' glass,

No bottom I could see, for

After emancipation, there was only

An Endless swamping Me.

Ferdinando raised the pipe to her. They smoked for a good
while saying nothing the lifefull Quiet Nature 'round them.

FERDINANDO
(*internal*)

This crestfallen, grimma[2] woman of love's swamp

Might drain my woes. If for boredom's slake…

If James Joiner will not join to widow,

Why, then let her marry Ferdinando!

---

[1] paraphrasing a couplet of John Donne's

[2] grim; frightful

*Marigold devoured the dish of otter and drank the moonshine
that shone there for Ferdinando could concoct such spirits.*

FERDINANDO

Madam, his spurn of you is to me, spur,

It maddens me that this maiden beauty

Would not my misery master en-madden,

It stokes my soul like this piping pipe-smoke,

Hem! It hips my hammock into a hell!

I cannot stand to sit on it!

*He stood stomped circled and sat beside Marigold. He
generously allowed her to lean her head on his shoulder.*

FERDINANDO

I think you've met our James' otherguise,

I've known him a long time: he has sides' two,

A summer, a winter, sat on same tree,

These two timbers that match, spar as at a match

Of lawn bowling, a bumbler playing self,

Rolls 'fouls', or knocks lucky 'any old hows',

Obsessed with his fool game his, friends neglects.

He sidled closer to her.

FERDINANDO

Picture this bowler at play on his lawn,

Joying or groaning at pins, what's behind?

Marry, tis his married wife, she's inhouse

Worked to the elbow's grease feeding their babes,

Cleaning their cabinets, kitchens, and clutter

Of her idling husband's bowled blunders,

Suffer suffers she under stutters of

Tumbling pins. What is a wife to do…?

He leaned very close hip to hip.

FERDINANDO

Why, she has a gardener, who she knows

Her garden beds he tends to flowery shows,

Well, why not invite him in for a spell?

To clean… or cook… or monitor slob babes.

While her minim man games outside,

Perhaps, the gardener tends to flower the bedside.

He attempted a kiss. Shocked she pulled away.

MARIGOLD MAMMON

Oh wicked servant! Oh unfaithful slave!

FERDINANDO

I am not James' slave!

MARIGOLD MAMMON

His knave, knife in back!

He will hear of this from me, Marigold!

FERDINANDO

Jamestown! Hear, James' and Jamestown! A

wicked

Widow of dismal, great swamp this way comes

To re-haunt you!

MARIGOLD

Shut up!

FERDINADO

No, you!

MARIGOLD

No, you!

So they repeated that argument, which is hardly worth recording, as they raced back towards Jamestown.

Along the way they pass the Prospector who had made his own Jamestown on a wee hill in the swamp: a shack in miniature the tavern under which is buried a wax doll. The Prospector watched the raging couple run by he leaned down whispered what he'd seen to his doll without a why.

BERKELEY'S MANSION – EVENING

A small stage. A torn red curtain. It parts: Iostaf, in the shape of the Guardsman, thespianish, bows to Governor Berkeley:

GUARDSMAN

Governor, perform begins with James,

That wealthy man, that succeeder to smoke,

Smolders a smoker soon his smoke becomes,

He fumes for war! I saw him hand in hand

With a burning brand, with burning Bacon,

98

Who stunk of brimstone, sulfur, and corpses' lime,

And with cloven hoofs, and cuck horns atop[1],

Danced into plantation to devil's time.

On the stage mimes of Nathaniel Bacon and his lackeys and
a James Joiner enter carrying dead pigs which they roast on
long lead spits. Great bonfires. Garlands. Two widows.
Guns. Grog.

GUARDSMAN

Hyena laughers they such revel made,

That upon my constant shape I do swear

I saw Satan himself ope' up the lid

Of his coffin, peeling back the earth with

All his demoniacs and Pan himself

Upon flute, as torrent undammed the damned

Flowed in carouse, or galloped like mad mounts,

And charged from breach to breach,

They rammed themselves into the revelry!

The mime of James Joiner he began a drinking contest with
the Pan collapsing on the sixth swallow. The winner the Pan
danced his way all the way to the moon shining in the
blue midnight (made to seem real on the stage).

---

[1] horns, a common symbol of both devil and cuckold

GUARDSMAN

But not all was as image mere, hectic

Of bonfire, all heat with no hot's burning,

For not afar after this James' collapse,

That Nathaniel Bacon like a god rose,

Approached, and bid him wake from his low nod,

As some shifting savior, he unbed'ed James

Of the cold ground's grave, like a Lazarus

He raised, but to Ministry nefarious,

For then assembled, parables of men,

Crow-scares impaled on staves implanted

In the ground, stood in a line and costumed

Like these mimes here in the faux shifts and face

Of your very soldiers, Governor, O'! List…

They soon I saw brought out the tallest, leanest

Scarecrow – was in the shape of you yourself.

They did this also on the stage recreating the crime scene.

GUARDSMAN

When this strange trome[1] of standers straw were led

Into their line, their executioners

Marched to formations of faux murder,

With firearms, and James as their very chief,

They readied, raised, leveled, and booming shot!

---

[1] a band of soldiers

The actors fire the faux bang of their guns. The scarecrows dressed as all the Governor & all the Governor's men explode in squibs of pigs' blood.

GUARDSMAN

Without hesitation, with total prejudice,

They your aspect butchered, cut, and consumed.

So ended what was scene, in blood and dance.

The scarecrow of the Governor is filled with food. The actors they eat & dance in rings 'round. All fades to quiet. Close the torn red curtain.

GOVERNOR BERKELEY
(*afraid*)

These dissenters we must now dissunder,

These revelers their revels bring to end,

Their embering rebellion souse to silence.

They think themselves twin to us to twine us,

Times invert on such inversions…

Guardsman! Arrest this James!

GUARDSMAN

Aye, tis done sir! I on the stoop of thy

Mansion found the man sat. Behold the man!

The Guardsman presented James Drugger bound gagged confounded yelling through the rag stomping his feet pleading with his eyes his self-assured innocence.

GOVERNOR BERKELEY

Well seen my eyes to find this black raven

Perched like death on my stoop. To gaol he'll go!

To church I and mine, keep me in the keep!

For our stone church of power is our seat.

James Drugger that man wealthy in smoke he's thrown into

the jail. He sits on straw and stone floors. He wails his fate.

The Guardsman watched him from above changes to Iostaf.

IOSTAF
(*aside*)

So our story's sloped to land on a jail,

But worry not, this James shall have his bail,

For a brother will soon his brother find,

That's inevitable, their orbits're aligned,

For I hear on the horizon the fight

Of Widow and Maroon their midnight flight

Will traject' them to this fetter of James,

So read on, I've not yet ended our games!

But this was the end of Act 3…

ACT 4

JAMESTOWN CHURCH – DAWN

The bare winter morning. The midnight snows have left their glaze on ground and branches and boughs to glitter and go under the sun. The white blank is peacefull everywhere.

The mob's blazing brands. The mob's black hats. The guns of the mob glittering under the same light.

Nathaniel Bacon, his men (freemen, servants, black slaves, two widows) & James Joiner all disheveled hungry hungover marched to Jamestown's church. They want the Governor.

Governor Berkley and his men are inside talking about what to do about Bacon.

Bacon surrounded them. James Joiner ran up to the church.

> JAMES JOINER
> (*knocking on the door*)
>
> Knock knock in the name of the President!
>
> GOVERNOR BERKLEY
>
> Yes, just a moment please!

JAMES JOINER

Of course, of course!

James Joiner like a jolly dog lopes back to Bacon to sit by his
side to wait for his Governor Berkley to come out the church.

JAMES JOINER

Perhaps this bumpkin Berkley won't will out?

NATHANIEL BACON

He will; he won't a challenge un-answer.

But they waited till the torches dimmed.

JAMES JOINER
(*impatient*)

Manalive! Nate, when I was a shipboy

Off the shoals of Blackpool, and indeed all

The world's anchoring's, many a'friendly box

We made under the jib, some not so sport

When harpoon and holystone[1] were wielded,

But if you catch my fish, not one melee

Couldn't be mended by a splice of main brace[2]...

That is to say, anger'll be snuffed in sack[3].

NATHANIEL BACON

When were you ever in England, James Drugger?

---

[1] a disk used to swab the deck; the sailors' disputes
apparently steeled in imitation of a knightly combat
[2] alcohol

[3] sherry sack, a Spanish wine

104

JAMES JOINER

But I'm not drugging you, crisp Sir Bacon,

I'm just saying that I'm not a crack shot,

And if this revolution comes to more

Than a knock of knuckles, I might have seen

Too much of the elephant[1], and might

Flee the general muster.

NATHANIEL BACON

Deserters will be shot-

JAMES JOINER
(*frightened; stuttering*)

-Mustard! I mean to say I'd I'd flee the

General frolic to to return! Yes, return

And resupply any needs the brave comrades

Might need like mustard for fueling the gut

Of our workers! Or keep their powders dry

With my sleeves, or wet proletariat sweat, I mean

Their foreheads dab with m-my, nervous tears, oh

my-

-Enter, Governor Berkley arrayed in all the armors of a knight of old: a pot helmet a mailed coif a meshy visor rusty plates his heraldry: a heart between two roses gules on a black field.

---

[1] idiomatic – I have got more than I bargained for

All stand in shock. Berkely creaks forward wearing the wide white hat atop his helm. Bacon put on his wide black hat. Berkely creaks up to Bacon his arms wide in greeting.

GOVERNOR BERKELEY

Nathan, Nathaniel Bacon, my Nate,

What are your demands, why have you come so

Armed with so many arms?

NATHANIEL BACON

We free men-

TWO WIDOWS

-And two widows!

NATHANIEL BACON

And two widows

Do demand the right to fare war! We seek

A commission, to conquest and plunder

The lands of loathsome Indians, to perform

Our noble butchery, gentle burnings,

Chivalric looting, and merciful exterminations.

THOMAS TOOKER

Oh! And the pillaging, sir, don't forget!

JENKIN PRICE

And the theft....

THOMAS TOOKER

That's what pillaging is.

JENKIN PRICE

Is it?

GOVERNOR BERKELEY

Your claim to commission I do

Rightly deny, to Bacon and all here panned.

But as I see the formations of your arms,

And assume you make your claim by armed force,

So I will meet the face of force with face.

Nathaniel Bacon, I knightly challenge

To single combat's duel, a knightly tourney

Today will decide the day. Face me.

Governor Berkley drew his sword.

NATHANIEL BACON

Nay.

*Berkley felt insulted and so he offered his bared breast to him
(after removing his plate armor which took quite a while).*

GOVERNOR BERKELEY

Here! Shoot me, foregod, here's fair mark, shoot

me![1]

NATHANIEL BACON

No, may it please your honor, we will not hurt

A hair of your head, nor of any other man's,

---

[1] this an almost direct quote from Berkley, taken from
an eye and ear witness' account

We are come for a commission to save

Our lives from the Indians, which you have so

Often promised, and now we will have it

Before we go.

So at gunpoint the commission to wield guns was penned and ratified. Bacon could begin his legal march on the murderous Indian men, women, and children. Bacon bid his mob home.

Enter, Marigold Mammon and Ferdinando, hot and heavy and muddy and full of swamp.

FERDINANDO

Jamestown! Hear, James' of Jamestown! the
  wicked

Widow of the swamp re-haunts you!

MARIGOLD

Shut up!

FERDINADO

No, you!

MARIGOLD

No, you!

They bump into James Joiner, parting him from his mob's march.

MARIGOLD

James!

JAMES JOINER

Marigold!

FERDINANDO

James!

(*noticing his gun*)

Oh…

JAMES JOINER

What ho, Ferdinand-

(*noticing his swamp*)

-Oh…

Pause.

MARIGOLD

James, you must know all the wicked deceits

Of this serpent servant, cook-up of putdowns who

Abandons his betters, brings up bridges

Of aid to deceive confessions out me a

Lost and lonely widow-

JAMES JOINER

-What happened, love?

MARIGOLD

Ha! Love!? I don't understand you, James of

change,

But list, lost in the great dismal rude swamp

I came to this Maroon asking him aid,

And made desperate pleas for alma alms

109

So famished I was for hunger and feeling,

And no sooner were vitals and comfort

To me given, than this wicked Maroon,

This slave to his appetite lust alone,

Made his advance on me, to conquest me,

As a defenseless hamlet would to all

The swords and long spears of the great Kahn bow.

But I didn't yield but fled!

JAMES JOINER

Ferdinando!

Explain this town sacking.

FERDINANDO
(bemused)

James, like a widow of some skill she's spun

All her spidery threads into this yarn

To catch and lead her Theseus by ear,

When out labyrinth, she at entrance will pounce,

For there she leers above like a black widow

To string him up, catch him ever on her Crete.

This swamp ponk's Minotaur and Ariadne!

Monstrous bright deceiver, who wears all her

Mammon modesty as false as fool's gold,

To shine in eyes her glitters, attracting

Your growing reach! But beware to grab on

Her back'd treasure'd nothing, for grip gripes back-

110

-Marigold slaps Ferdinando into the black wintery mud.

JAMES JOINER

I stand the best man at the marriage,

Ferdinando the feculent to his bride: mud.

James picked him up from the ground.

FERDINANDO

Her slap's like Jove's thunderclaps!
JAMES JOINER
(*taking her hand*)

Aye, but her kiss

Is Venus, the wave foam's gentle laps.

Now tell what's really happened.

FERDINANDO

Well, James, as I'd said I thought this Bacon

A barking bandog of the blood moon night,

And displeased with his sway on you, and your

Crude diss of me, and your spoiled attitude

Which seemed to begird you like a wide hoop,

Pushing off all friends from orbit, I

Started my angle to reel you back from foolery,

Thinking there in my swamp I'd wind my bait,

Pondering, angling, aging,

But not long at leisure I in-hammock'd lay,

When this beldam of damn's diss emergéd

111

From the muck and the mire, beslubberéd
In sus green garb, pond hat, and algae muffs,
Which so frighted me, that from hammock I fell
At speeds breakneck, but seeing she'was woman,
And no more malicious than love could make,
I took generous pities upon her,
Fed her with my cackerel stew, watered
Her with my heavenly storehouses
Of moonshine caught in cups, and indeed let
Her bathe herself in my bark fashioned tub,
A suave you can see she's now re-sullied.

She was messy from the swamp run, but so was Ferdinando.

FERDINANDO

After the alms'd fermented, she made much
Complaint to me of your conduct, saying
That you neglected her, and abandoned
Her embrace for the snout of rebel swine,
And she said your kiss game was poor, more like
Smack of stony wall's chink than lover's lips,
As more insults she shoveled on of you,
Her body closer to me disclosed, touching,
Bracing my hand like an armlet slip'd down,
Toying with the hills and lines of my palms,
As a predicting chiromancer bespeaks

A rising morning, a tumbling night, last,

With her heart palpitating apitpat

Unto my lips she leaned

And sieged the breach

With kiss.

MARIGOLD

This was his wish more than his history.

James Joiner bemused simply smiled nodded & hand in hand
led them both down a snowy alleyway.

JAMES JOINER

This I do say to both of you at once,

I find this dapper run and talk the top

Of charm, it does melt the glacier of my heart,

For this anger's fire is of love's kindling's,

And I do warm both my hands equally

By both your flames, for I do love you each.

First he addressed Ferdinando:

JAMES JOINER

Know that when you fled from me in anger,

Like some wounded stag, that I as any

Love's hunter would, did pursue you, but was

Diverted by my master, Bacon, but rest

Assured the chase I would have re-footed.

Second he addressed his maid Marigold:

JAMES JOINER

Now my Marigold, my soon to be bride,

Unwidowed wife, I know you are distraught

That the time was too long to return me,

But delay was for me to find the best

Wedding ring no eye has seen nor ear heard!

MARIGOLD
(*incredulous*)

Oh yes? Is that so?

JAMES JOINER

Yes, may I not be

Your James if that's not so.

MARIGOLD

Then this ring show.

JAMES JOINER

Mhm. Hm? Sorry?

MARIGOLD

Then this ring show!

A loss for words.

FERDINANDO
(*looking up; improvising*)

How does one hear a wedding ring, my James?

A bell from the church rang out.

114

JAMES JOINER

Ha! Hear! Fortune's freedom rings out for me!

I am the luckiest man in Virginia!

Then James Joiner was arrested.

He was hauled away despite the discourses of Ferdinando the slaps of Marigold who both received some swift blows from sticks and were thus driven off for a time.

THE JAILHOUSE – LATE MORNING

There was one cell for all prisoners. There James Drugger incarcerated with the following:

Three Native Amerikan children (disobedience in the White schools), an old woman tailor (pricking), two black slaves (concupiscence), and one Thomas Ratt (failure to pay a debt of one guilder for the purchase of a squaw's herbal aphrodisiac, jimsom roots, and several beads of wampum on knotted string).

The prisoners play dominos with pebbles, sticks, teeth and old bones.

James Drugger sits sulking in the corner. He bangs his shoe on the bars of the cell.

JAMES DRUGGER

Guard! Guard!

GUARDSMAN

Yes, James?

JAMES DRUGGER

Guard, guard, give me water.

GUARDSMAN

(*handing him a cow's hoof*)

Aye, sir, here sir.

JAMES DRUGGER

Guardsman…

GUARDSMAN

Yes, sir?

JAMES DRUGGER

This' a hoof.

GUARDSMAN

(*looking at it to make sure*)

Yes, it is sir.

JAMES DRUGGER

I ask you for water

And you give me a hoof?

GUARDSMAN

Yes, I did sir.

JAMES DRUGGER

Well why did you give me a hoof?

GUARDSMAN

Yes sir,

Well sir my ol' Nuncle once had a blaze,

A flaming on his cow fence sir.

JAMES DRUGGER

Yes… and?

GUARDSMAN

'And', sir?

JAMES DRUGGER

What does this cow fence a'flame have to do

With a hobbled off old cow's hoof, sir? Eh, sir!?

GUARDSMAN

Well t'was what he did with the hoof sir-

JAMES DRUGGER

-Well what did he do with the hoof sir, eh!?

GUARDSMAN

Oh! Well he unhoofed the cow first, and at

The flaming fence, sir, he threw the hoof

JAMES DRUGGER

And???

GUARDSMAN

Put the fire out.

James Drugger shrugged his shoulders and slumped down.
The Guardsman sat beside him on the other side of the bars.

GUARDSMAN

Well sir, what puts out fire?

JAMES DRUGGER

Not a bloody hoof!

GUARDSMAN

Nay sir, t'was bloody after the unhoofing.

JAMES DRUGGER

No, no! Water! Water puts out the fire!

GUARDSMAN

Indeed sir, and as this hoof's put out my ol'

    Nuncle's

Fire, and as water puts out fire, so I would say that

This hoof is water, and so you've got a gift a'water.

James Drugger facepalmed and groaned.

JAMES DRUGGER

I am guarded by a half-wit-

GUARDSMAN
*(standing; hopping up and down on
one leg; kicking the bars)*

-Nay sir,

Guarded by a half-feet you are, a shifting uniped!

Hahaha!

James Drugger slumped further down the wall.

GUARDSMAN
(*sitting back down; friendly*)

What did the fish say when it hit the wall?

JAMES DRUGGER

I don't care.

GUARDSMAN

Nay sir, he didn't say that. The fish said: Dam.

JAMES DRUGGER

…Let heaven take me to thy silent bosom…

Elsewhere in the cell Thomas Ratt loses the round and curses with rolling r's as one of the Native Amerikan children lines up a full train of dominoes and rides it to the forests of the West where the wind flows through the black hair.

GUARDSMAN
(*massaging James' back*)

Why did the blind man tumble down into the well?

JAMES DRUGGER

Oh why? Why me??

GUARDSMAN

Nay sir, that's not why. Why was, the blind man,
He couldn't see that well.

JAMES DRUGGER

…Why do you torment me?

GUARSMAN

Merry sir, I do mean to remake you,

For you've lost not your wits but your wit's whip,

Not your head but your headiness, which 'ternal

Is compared to but a putt neck. Listen,

Here's a last happy tale, tis about you.

Once there was an old bellman in ol'belltower,

Every morning he'd go on up to bell,

And he'd bob and smack his head against it,

For he had no hands to clap with, that's truth,

And he got terrible aches of head, but hell,

That bell, rang and rang true every Sunday,

Until one day he hit it so hard he

Knocked himself out, down and out he fell,

The next day, his brother visited the coroner,

And his brother was a total twin to'him,

Armless too, and coroner asks him, the twin,

Do you recognize this man? The twin,

He says, 'No, but his face sure rings a bell!'

JAMES DRUGGER

Leave me be, I'll sleep.

He does. A bell rings at the door.

Enter James Joiner and the three guardsmen.

THE THREE GUARDSMEN

Guardsman!

GUARDSMAN

Guardsmen!

THE THREE GUARDSMEN

Guardsman, this man's escaped.

GUARDSMAN

Well you'd best hop on catchin' him then,

guardsmen.

THE THREE GUARDSMEN

No, we mean he's already escaped, and we mean

He's escaped from this cell here. So, look on him.

Do you know this man?

The Guardsman looked James Joiner up-down very intently.

GUARDSMAN
(*confidently*)

No.

THE THREE GUARDSMEN

Well, by order of the Governor Berkley

He is to be incarcerated now here.

GUARDSMAN

Alright!

They handed James Joiner into his custody.

THE THREE GUARDSMEN
(*as they exit*)

Guardsman.

GUARDSMAN

Guardsmen!

The Guardsman led James Joiner into the cell and sat him opposite of James Drugger, who was far too depressed to look up, as James Joiner paced excitedly about, played dominos, won a few rounds, lost more rounds.

The Guardsman snored slept dreaming out the end of the Act his eyes closed.

ACT 5

JAMESTOWN JAIL – NIGHT

Enter, Ferdinando and Marigold sneaking in. They came to the bars and hailed James Joiner to them not of course noticing James Drugger his back to them a 'slump and dozing and depressed.

MARIGOLD

James, we mean to break you out,

FERDINANDO

I've a plan!

Hearing her voice, James Drugger looked over. With James Joiner's back to him, James Drugger snuck over to listen.

JAMES JOINER

The worst of bars is what bars me from thee,

O' my Marigold, would this cell but an

Altar become, and these welded rods change

To the chains of our wedding vows-

MARIGOLD

- Enough, James, these words love I've heard

enough,

This' all: We mean to break you out of jail.

I'll not hear any else. Your love's unconstant-

JAMES JOINER

-Kiss me.

So he did through the bars. Look the other James (and Ferdinando both) blush.

JAMES DRUGGER
(*in jealousy*)

Now I see the widow's plot's exploded

To all its little parts! All scheming flames

Of Marigold burst on me a clarity!

MARIGOLD & FERDINANDO
(*jumping back in fright*)

Ah!

JAMES DRUGGER

So this knave was your knack all along,

You would wed me, cuck me with he,

Let out lands, fill the beds, full the coffers,

En-coffin this husband in earth for a

Younger churl-

JAMES JOINER

-Get back, thou jobbernowl[1]!

The two James' see themselves & jump backwards in terror.

THE TWO JAMES'

Ahhh!!!

They then in strange sequence each other's movements mirror: four hands up two hands held out two arms waving legs leaning shaking a left feet a tilting heads of one puzzled face.

FERDINANDO
(*to Marigold, whispering*)

We're in the middle of a mirror…

This perhaps explains the causes of our

Confusion, yet confusion's causations'

More a muddle than map.

Lady, I'll interrogate these type-twos.

The two James' continue to marvel at themselves.

FERDINANDO

You two of the too two! De-couple self

---

[1] a stupid person; a block head

From its self-locked sphere, answer out to me,

For self from itself must divorce, if speech's

To occur like persons, first, name your I's.

THE TWO JAMES'

I'm James!

FERDINANDO

Divide, I conjure thee, to full names!

JAMES JOINER

James Joiner!

JAMES DRUGGER

James Drugger!

FERDINANDO

Where and to whom

Were you born, James', answer in order spoke!

JAMES JOINER

Ferdinando, tis me you know, that I

Was born in Bristol, sired to a mother

Named Rebecca, but by poverty's Lethe pot

All my memory of her was forgot,

Vanished a vapor 'pon the glass of time,

Save for the knowing of her name, stamped

To me by the orphanage I escaped.

FERDINANDO

Thee I know indeed. Now, other, express.

JAMES DRUGGER

Now hear my origin as I was told

By my ish-father, great Gordon Drugger,

May he rest in peace... I was also in

Bristol born of woman Rebecca named.

His tale of my taking he did to me

Once relate, akin to Isaac's kin as

He said, for he caught me by my slight heel

When I fell from womb, before my other

Brother was birthed to rags of poverty.

The Guardsman the prisoners all listen very intently to this.

JAMES DRUGGER

Now my father was a mariner to his

Majesty's bidding, and not well bid for

His work he was, this to say he was poor,

And as he was not lover but brother

To my mother, he swore to adopt *one*

Of the unlucky urchins... I being

The first to fall into the savory

Venison of this world of death, t'was I,

I was by that father figure chosen,

While my other was to Church sacred'd,

He blessed me with expensive passage 'cross

Atlantic flood, over the watery ruins

We sailed, for years we sailed, from port to port,

Such was his trade while I bandy'd, sea mad, that

Mother was that treacherous, endless deep,

My world the stars and the sea and the ship,

My wet nurse was a sailor's goat,

    (the Guardsman guffaws)

My tales of times past and history of

The world were what could be read in heavens,

Or caught from companions' mouths sea legends,

What knowledges I got, fastened in mine ears,

None more enchanting than tales of New World,

So were my boyhood hopes most startled

When Gordon a plot on New World purchased,

And when on New World we landed… there was

A wilderness leapt from my dreams more strange,

More frightening, more quickening to mind

Than any my imagination might make…

The very trees were not yet named, stranger

Hills, and babbling brooks yet be language'd,

Like a boy I bounded through garden'new,

Singing to myself, naming for myself

All I saw… But this was not long to be.

Serpents (up from the sea) their slithers here,

The Red Men, already were in our world,

Already curled in boughs above, below…

127

Attempts to cultivate and civilize

The land savage and the savages there

Did only to rouse the savageness' in us,

For all toil and wars of ancient first Fall

Curséd goes on two feet…

Gordon Drugger this lesson learned when by

A serpent's sting he knew the end of all Thing,

Fall grounded him on an arrow's tip.

But he being a pragmatic man, he

A tobacco plantation first planted,

So grew his wealth in leaf and the black smoke,

Not the prosperity he planned but the one

That bought us life, more life, and living space.

Those gains were got to me on his death-day,

Which now shouts to me I am double blessed…

I thought upon occasion of my passed

Over brother, on how he might have fared,

On how he in England still lived, or passed

Over he passed away…

His name, his face, I never till now knew.

The listeners they take his words in. Quiet a moment.

GUARDSMAN

Why were you arrested?

FERDINANDO

My next question.

James Drugger straightened his back and huffed.

JAMES DRUGGER
(*to Guardsman*)

You know as well as I how imprisoned,

For this' the jesting pickthank that 'prisoned.

On what cause, I don't know.

FERDINANDO
(*to Guardsman*)

Well, why was the doppel[1] jot into jail?

GUARDSMAN

Tis no cursive, swart sir, he's arrested for

conspiracy,

A revolution raged 'gainst our good governor

Berkeley.

JAMES JOINER

Then this is indeed my brother my twin,

For I also willed our Bacon to win!

JAMES DRUGGER

Strangest fate! My accused was my accuser!

Guardsman, now you must let me be free,

For I'm not allied to that black baked pork,

But to Berkeley made my alliance, thus

---

[1] a ghostly double of a living person; an evil twin

129

The traitor was the trick of eying twins,

And am innocent I.

JAMES JOINER

You're with Berkeley?

JAMES DRUGGER

And you're with Bacon, the scarefire, stirrer

Of pot of people 'gainst their better dishing.

You're the spoiler of my face and name,

The soilure of my father's garden plot,

My plantation by birthright got, trickster

To this lonely widow, who's impertinent

Pecks I see were trice of your trickery.

JAMES JOINER

Ha! I am shocked.

JAMES DRUGGER

Guardsman, release me now.

Let the traitor stink in his tank-

FERDINANDO

-Wait. Listen, an angel would speak into this cell.

Marigold now comes forward.

MARIGOLD

(*to James Joiner*)

So it was you who wooed… was it true?

James Joiner glanced to Ferdinando, who nodded to him.

JAMES JOINER

True, true and true, my love, maid Marigold,

From first handshake hit by love was I struck,

Though to some deception I will admit,

These were the all's fair tricks of war in love,

And had no other end than you to wed.

JAMES DRUGGER

I suspect, Marigold, that my brother,

Bacon's poor porkling, is a bonded serf,

By his poverty is indentured

For many perennity, that along with

His swart servant here, I think they did mean

To wed you for your wealth,

Wed them to wealth, steal liberty with stealth.

MARIGOLD

All duplicity undeparted has

Returned double fold, again I hear, in one face,

Two hearts, two truths, two lies.

JAMES DRUGGER

But believe me Marigold, my refusal

Has been constant as all the continent,

But now that I see you were deceived,

My once a stone heart is melted, unfreezed,

And Marigold, I'd marry you.

FERDINANDO

How noble.

JAMES JOINER

No Marigold, I'd marry you!

FERDINANDO

How quick!

They both held out their hands through the bars. Marigold
stepped back disturbed. She takes Ferdinando's hand.

FERDINANDO

(*internal*)

Oh dear, I do indeed this widow love.

But how to theft her affection back?

Hmm… There's a mirror in these times… Then tis'

Good that my pander's pushed the brothers James

To leap in league pon'her Marigold glitter,

Next, I'll divert their routes by othergates,

Puddle of politics'll sunder the prime mates,

Sullied the image of suitors both,

She'll think either choice the axe, then

I'll string my bow to target the widow,

And lance me there the blank…

The whole prison watched the show.

FERDINANDO
(*addressing both James*)

Marry, sirs, we must the maid marry to *one*,

But *one* pair can be ever accoupled,

And so I'll settle this brothers' dispute

As old as brotherhood itself, Adam's

Sons also fought for the founding of love,

So your offerings of love must now to love

Present and fill the presence with presents.

So, James… Joiner last born first talks.

JAMES JOINER

Marigold, I am a poor man, tis true,

So by poverty my chests're all emptied,

Not a coin lies in my coffers, but these

Emptiness' I hold out as open hands offered,

For this chest has room generous to hold all

The rich wealth of love's affection, which on

Your lips I've but set a few diamond kiss,

Doubloons more I'd jewel to deck my Queen's

    crown,

In my heart I'd your majesty enthrone,

All my strong arms swear to your divinity,

To this noble devotion I devote,

I kneel now low, to rise as your loyal

Knight of the wedding band, your true husband.

THE PRISONERS

Awe!

FERDINANDO

Very well wooed, now James Drugger, speak.

JAMES DRUGGER

You loved me once. And you read me right

When you read me rent - I was wounded,

And afraid of woman's love, difficult tis'

To love with love's wounds yet unhealed...

So pity a heart as wounded as mine

And be mine, and mend all of me

My heart's tearings, that grafted, we to we,

Will grow to greatness in tenderness,

With deep roots strong, of love to love wedded,

Grow the leaves of long life, branch's fidelity,

Patience's height, and the seeds of children

To grow after us, twins of our planted

And our well grown up love.

THE PRISONERS

Awe! That one was just as good. Twins in-deed!

FERDINANDO

Well, Marigold, is there yet a victor?

MARIGOLD

I'm flattered doubly but can't yet decide...

This may be two much for one heart to hear.

FERDINANDO

Then we'll dig deeper into this debate,

This pit of brother 'gainst brother pitted,

For the motes of love in each other's eye

Is each fecund, desire's here-both assured,

But are the beaming gazes yet ensured?

Then to James in their Jamestowns we'll look,

So tell me James, James... Drugger, when Bacon

Does his revolution win, what'll be the fate

Of fortune-inherited plantation?

JAMES DRUGGER
(*angry*)

No, Bacon will not this Jamestown usurp!

JAMES JOINER
(*angry*)

And wide-brimmed Berkley will be much better!?

He'd keep us free men in indentured slavery,

With no land, woman, emancipation,

A shame it is for an Amerikan to

A lash, a manacle, a master submit,

Or to a red Indian beg land-alms,

Or for other's purse spend his lifespan brief!

But Bacon will bring equality for all!

I say, *this* James' Jamestown's all for Bacon!

JAMES DRUGGER

Yet you're a slave to Bacon!

My pudder-kin, a head who our king's hand

Would cut with a snap, there's not a thought in you,

Heel clutching other, a heel clicking brother,

Thou goose stepping, marching soldier and dummy

Of all revolution's past and yet to be, thou-

JAMES JOINER

-More mud from the big mouth of my sad brooder!

JAMES DRUGGER

Ha! If my mouth is big then so is yours.

JAMES JOINER

I'll have you know I am no heel clicker

To an order-ers whistle!

JAMES DRUGGER

Yet still dog'd.

JAMES JOINER

You're for Berkley because Berkley's for you,

The rich will rip for rich! Like loves its likes!

GUARDSMAN

Yet he his mirrorlike steams to dislike!

All the jail were watching this exchange like a tennis match
their heads going back and forth from blow to blow.

JAMES DRUGGER

Ah ha! Now your hand's shown your royal flush!

For all the rich you would want drained, not for

A love of the poor or their plight but for

The burnings of envy in your heart, you'd

Not turn that envy energy around

Into honest work, that would wax you wealth,

As I've done, but you'd simply steal and take.

JAMES JOINER

You did not work for your waxéd white wealth!

You fat moons of father harvested months!

You were struck into Egypt already rich,

Drawn from waters of wealth to sat upon

A pharaoh's lap to suck on the dugs,

You've grown wide and grown fat against the losers

Of fortune's wheel, proud of pish[1] chance, yet

You, have, earned, nothing!

JAMES DRUGGER

Now I see… My twin's a pickthank…

You want me to buy you your freedom, eh?

And that of your black Pandarus[2] here, eh?

And give you both of my plot a portion?

Perhaps pay for your wedding my mistress?

---

[1] random; of poor quality
[2] a notorious bawd of Trojan War legend

Eh? Eh? She who you'd get by guise, my guise,

Me. Stealing my face. My name. My purse.

JAMES JOINER

The Marigold you discarded I saw

A diamond in this James' town muck,

JAMES DRUGGER

Diamonds!

Ha! Do you hear that? Ha! Diamonds indeed!

Her jewelry he'saw, indentured to money

You are oh twin of mine.

JAMES JOINER

No, no, no, now you see in me what's most in thee.

Tis your fixation's that's broke on money, not

beauty,

Otherwise your 'mistress' you'd have long ago

wed,

Long before *this* James on Jamestown you had

tread.

*Marigold stands distraught. The Guardsman mutters
something only she can hear:*

GUARDSMAN

Who-cooks-for-you, who-cooks-for-you-all…

MARIGOLD

(*in pain*)

Oh heart, I've heard you last…

FERDINANDO

(*to Marigold, gently*)

Marigold, we can walk out this open jail.

MARIGOLD

(*quietly*)

Gaol is got in me. By my own heart,

Divided two, shackled two, I imprisoned.

My heart was hab and nab and hurled

Me to tumult. And I do see now in

This cell this very heart's warring display,

As though a puppetry, behind the bars,

On marionette strings, my spirit danced

Her the dance of two sprites a'split.

This is love's show.

FERDINADO

Then let's both let it go.

Exit, Marigold, Ferdinando. The twins they do not notice.

JAMESTOWN – A SNOWY NIGHT

The town was full of fear. They locked themselves in.

They had heard that Bacon and his troop were not going to Indian territory but are marching on Jamestown tonight to behead the Governorship. The town is full of fear.

Tobacco smoke fumes through the boarded-up windows. No revelry. No lights. Cold. Dark. Snow falling in white slants.

Yet Marigold was pleased to feel the cold air to hear the general silence of the empty streets of Jamestown. Without word to Ferdinando but with him following she gadded slowly through Jamestown her eyes wandering into its blank windows or closed doors or down its drifting alleys.

At the church she stopped and gazed up at its steeple.

FERDINANDO

Marigold? Are you alright?

MARIGOLD

I'd say so.

I am going back to my plantation now.

She turned in that direction and walked there. Ferdinando followed. At the edge of town she stopped, faced him.

MARIGOLD

What do you want?

FERDINANDO

Well...

MARIGOLD

You too?

FERDINANDO

Marigold...

MARIGOLD

Leave be.

FERDINANDO

Marigold-

MARIGOLD

-Leave be.

NATHANIEL BACON

Tie them two!

Bacon's army had been camped there on the crossroads. They had come down to pillage the town. So the two not-lovers were tied with many knots hand to hand foot to foot their mouths stuffed and their faces stuck together by the side of the snowy road.

Bacon let them be.

The two, they got to work on losing their ropes.

As burning torches went down to Jamestown.

THE JAILHOUSE – MIDNIGHT

Now the James' had been arguing until they grew too tired to talk and so shunned each other sitting on opposite sides of the cell. James Drugger sat with Thomas Ratt while James Joiner sat with the others (see above) – who had taken his side of the argument.

Enter, John Pot. The Guardsman laughed ushered him in and led him to James Joiner.

THE GUARDSMAN

Is this your James?

JOHN POT

Yes, this' my servant, fit only for refunds.

JAMES JOINER

Oh my valiant master! Thanks be to

Heaven you've found me! Gracious, good, wide,

Just enough just, pursy gutted master,

To see you now am I so relieved!

Raise me up and I'll interpret your dreams!

For master's as awe-full as a pharaoh!

You may bargain for my release…

JOHN POT

Your shove of me shoved you into this jail.

James of Jail! O', there's justice in Jamestown!

JAMES JOINER

Ah! Shoved you?? No, that I would never do!

GUARDSMAN

Tis true that he's not imprisoned for push.

JOHN POT

What? Then what is the slave, er, servant, here for?

GUARDSMAN

Jailed for? Why, he befuddled himself for governor.

JOHN POT

Guardsman, I own this man's years… see here?

I've branded his ear. That's my sealed stamp.

Release him to me, and I will punish.

The Guardsman let open the gate. James Joiner winked at his

twin and waltzed out. James Drugger stomped to John Pot.

JAMES DRUGGER

The fat boat's been rigged right to sail again!

JOHN POT
(*stumbling back; falls on his stall*)

Ah! Devils! A doppler's dual haunt! Murder!

He rolled about a bit on his wheel.

JOHN POT

Guardsman! Help me!

JAMES JOINER

You know this boat, brother?

JAMES DRUGGER

Yes, this was she the SS Lard that would

Have made a slave of me, confused for thee,

Had not I shoved him onto his starboard.

JAMES JOINER

The boat is better sat stranded.

JAMES DRUGGER

Brother,

He's not seaworthy, he's a leaky boat,

143

His pox and pore let out all the scuttlebutt.
> JAMES JOINER

And he's barnacled, sluggish in the course.
> JAMES DRUGGER

His jobbernowl[1]'s his sail, lets out more wind
Than carries it in,
> JAMES JOINER

> He sucked up so the winds

Of trade along my way, the sea seemed dead!
> JAMES DRUGGER

Worse this, the boat stinks so, to sink in sea-
> JAMES JOINER

-Would so a relief to her sailors be!
> JAMES DRUGGER

Oh he's a cruel captain of his boat too!
> JAMES JOINER

Aye, he so hardly swabs his deck, that crabs-
> JAMES DRUGGER

-Rats, mollusks, and moles do dot all his planks.
> JOHN POT
> (*rolling about*)

Guardsman, hey ho, heaven's sake, raise me up!

---

[1] the flab of the upper neck

The Guardsman had changed into a pyramid eir head a point where the bright eye was. Ey sat immobile as the brother's berating intensified. Stage darkens. Stage strange's. Vision:

Look, the Jailhouse becomes a battlefield of Bunker Hill with the two James' joined in a colonist's coalition regimented together 'gainst their mutual oppressor John Pot who you can see has been changed into the shape of a great Britannic power the giant Albion rolling round on his greedy stomach moaning for tea and tax and wigs and the oppressor's permission.

Bravely did the Brothers James dressed in red blue and white mark valleys of lead through Giant Albion who writhed and rolled from his mouth spewed lobster-backs a'fire hurly-burly up the humpty hill firing yet futile the wager was for all the redcoat's eyes of white went red and rolled down Bunker Hill into mud that was by blood sown a soil'd Amerika.

Look, Nathaniel Bacon and his army – Whites and Blacks and boys into Jamestown charged falling on guards citizens slaves servants all. In blind revolutionary rage they set Jamestown alight forming an inferno – here's all hell'd – smokers their smoke become & flowed like smoke ebbing

*unto ash on the winter night, the night of pillage butchery
bewitching and vision.*

*Leaky John Pot. The James' boys fled their cage. They joined
the general revelry of rage of red. Pin her down, Jamestown.*

Alcohol, stored in the archives of the lawcourts, are opened.

Flowing.

Earth quakes!

*The tavern floor of Deaf John, it comes up like a crust. SAHM
rises from his slumber there strides a Giant guffawing &
free & stomping into the snowing forest fire night. Is gone.*

*Bacon's rebels freed all slaves and enslaved all masters.
They carry the drunk William Byrd, the alderman high above
their heads, a man-key, from door to door they carry him, the
keycarrier, to open all the doors to take, take, the tobacco the
drink and the trinket they find, house to house to red tinder
to rubble to wrecks to late into the morning that rose maroon
and Blessed this*

The Amerikan Revolution of 1676

With sin and sun.

JAMESTOWN – THE SUNRISE

We wandered through the memory of Jamestown. Revelers slept on beds of ash. The snow covered the ash. Adam Thorngood his walking stick clicked on the stones of the ruin. He walked to the top of the toppled church steeple.

ADAM THORNGOOD

Our revolution was but a stumble

Into rubble. And our Amerika,

Begun upon a con, almost ended

In this event of a black swan, for while

The times of starvation, the Indian

Invasions, and even such feudalism

Our Amerika survived, could not an

Internal schism abide, for only an

Amerika by Amerikans may die.

A servant woman under the stones. He carried away the stones he carried the woman laid her on the soft ash the fresh snow. He snapped his fingers a bonfire beside her revived her. He changed to Iostaf.

IOSTAF

So also by eirself may save eirself,

Amerika by Amerikans birth,

Burgeon unto a Blessing without

A bound at all. From out this heap of ruin'd
Rubble, I'd pull a People.

Nathaniel Bacon was lying low in the bones of Deaf John's
tavern, drunk, shivering, dying of dysentery, fading away.

IOSTAF

Was this the man I chose to make this Nation?
Or is he but pre-figure of some other,
A much better-blesséd brother? If so,
Then this revolution was but sizzle,
Of a burning Bacon by father's face
Downcast so cast down his gauntlet to ground
To make war on his patrial Berkley,
He stoked the heart of hatred and envy
Against the rich and so-called Red. Bacon,
He made himself the very character
Of charisma, crowned himself the first
Of Kings Amerika, kneeled on faldstool [1]
Of low tavern bench, and reigned pestilence
On this land like a flood falling to drench.

Iostaf, ey shakes eir head in pity. Ey turns aside from Bacon.

---

[1] a low stool, humbly kneeled on by kings or queens
during their coronations

IOSTAF

I'll wend the time for the better brother.

Rebelling Bacon will yet die low death,

Bleeding out all his ends his red life's lux[1],

Bacon will die of body's bloody flux[2].

So vigor of all men comes to an end,

Borns, burns, reaches, yet their funerals attend.

Ey turns to Berkley hiding in a boat under his wide white hat.

IOSTAF

All onlookers will be looked on laid low!

Berkeley to his Jamestown will yet return,

To put down the remnant rebellion dwindled

To but eighty and twenty servants and slaves,

These hundred freedom fighters, dregs humane,

To the masters of men will be re-chained,

And Berkeley all his taken he'll re-took,

And more than that he'll took, for to tyranny

He himself'll be pushed, and like his Bacon

Become, gallows' boards be let to fall

Before his re-plunder's be at end at all,

Hangman's job's steady, till my Berkley

---

[1] light; the spirit of life

[2] the revolutionary Nathaniel Bacon died of dysentery on October 26, 1676

149

Will to England be recall'd, in England

Interred, in terra grave, half a'world away

From New World's kingly sway,

Like the sun, does rise but to set in a day.[1]

Ey wandered to the bound' of the dust.

IOSTAF

So what then became of the brothers James?

I hear they saw a vision, in plundering fray,

And on this very day rose to deed as

Truefriends, accoupled in the butchering

Of John Pot, who seemed swelled to giant,

Was gargantuan felled by cannon shot.

By their victory, grown in confidence,

Unto mist mantled mountains Appalachian

Did frontier, arm in brotherly arm,

For fronts to find, gadding to spread

The fame, riches, and prize of giant-felling,

They did found a spot, not near a pox-swamp,

But by an ancient spring and hoary frith[2],

Hills with minerals, diamonds, gold, and lead

Might fund next revolution yet to be led.

---

[1] Berkley dies on the 9th of July 1677 in England,
after again becoming Governor of Jamestown.
[2] ancient forest; peaceful

By the bones of that Giant John Pot

They planted, as cillín[1], a foundation

For a frontier town, which they did christen,

What else but 'A Town of James'?

Ey showed in a mirror the image of the shanty shady
mountain town populated by the two brothers. Twelve slaves,
and three servants were working there under them. They are
in the Waxhaws[2].

IOSTAF

Look, the first of the crop was tobacco,

For that leaf must grow, its smoke must flow!

Crash! Iostaf eir mirror ey smashed...

IOSTAF

All that's quaking to be born will be so... but

What of widow and her Ferdinando?

This' the last I'll show.

THE GREAT DISMAL SWAMP –
EVENING

Ferdinando and Marigold had freed themselves of their
bonds. Marigold's plantation had turned to smoke. So she &

---

[1] a home built above the burial of a child
[2] this Amerikan region, in South Carolina territory,
would later birth one Andrew Jackson

Ferdinando fled into the Swamp, lowered the drawbridge, crossed it together. He let her have his hut.

His family becomes hers.

He gave her his blanket and wished her goodnight and left her to sleep alone. One night she came to him.

Hear, under the bride's house was another sleeper, another Giant. That very night, she dreamed of things that were to come of her conceiving country, an Amerika, lovers in love's intwine, on her face, the gentlest smile for the coming time.

THE SWAMP – AFTERNOON

Iostaf wandered among swamp, going with the glowing will-o'-the-wisps. Ey wandered to the foot of an old Hickory tree.

IOSTAF

So our first book of Amerika ends,

A storm of feeling to a calm of friends,

Thanks for reading, for there's made my living,

But now I dwindle down to darks of sleep,

To sleep until a next narrate giving,

Then as a happy morning's wake I'd leap

To tell the next tale of our History

Of Amerika slant

Blazed on tongues poet'd cant…

Ey lay in the tree and yawned and closed eir eyes and swayed.

IOSTAF

Let the last page of Amerika's first

Be turned, let all readers yearn with a thirst

For more, that into their ears I may pour,

The very silver of the mirror mind, so

To their image own be ever spellbind...

Ey fell asleep. Exeunt omnes.

Close the curtains two.

SOME HISTORICAL SOURCES

B.A., Botkin. *A Treasury of American Folklore. 2.* Guilford: Globe Pequot, 2016. Print.

David Brion, Davis and Steven Mintz. *The Boisterous Sea of Liberty. 2.* Oxford, New York: Oxford University Press, 1999. Print.

Dee, Brown. *Bury My Heart at Wounded Knee. 2.* New York: Henry Holt and Company , 2007. Print.

Edmund S, Morgan. *American Slavery, American Freedom. 2.* New York, London: WW Norton & Company, 2003. Print.

Frederick Jackson, Turner. *The Significance of the Frontier in American History.* Mansfield Centre: Martino Publishing, 2014. Print.

Richard, Erdoes and Alfonso Ortiz. *American Indian Myths and Legends.* New York: Pantheon Books, 1984. Print.

Coming soon…

Joseph Eldredge's next book!

The Books of Amerika, Book II

An Andrew Jackson

Will be available at

choicepublications.org

breathofalmighty.org

Amazon,

Barnes & Noble

Booksellers around the globe!